IN THE DESERT OF DESIRE

IN THE DESERT OF *Desire*

LAS VEGAS AND THE CULTURE OF SPECTACLE

WILLIAM L. FOX

UNIVERSITY OF NEVADA PRESS / RENO & LAS VEGAS

This book has been funded, in part, by a grant from the Nevada Arts Council, a state agency, and the National Endowment for the Arts, a federal agency.

University of Nevada Press, Reno, Nevada 89557 USA

Manufactured in the United States of America
Design by Carrie House / HOUSEdesign llc
Library of Congress Cataloging-in-Publication Data
Fox, William L., 1949–
In the desert of desire : Las Vegas and the culture of spectacle /
William L. Fox.
p. cm.
Includes bibliographical references and index.
ISBN 0-87417-563-1 (hardcover : alk. paper)
1. Las Vegas (Nev.) —Cultural policy. 2. Las Vegas (Nev.) —
Civilization. 3. Popular culture—Nevada—Las Vegas. 4. Arts—
Nevada—Las Vegas. 5. Art museums—Nevada—Las Vegas.
6. Zoos—Nevada—Las Vegas. 7. Dance companies—Nevada—
Las Vegas. I. Title.
F849.L35F694   2005
306.4'7'09793135—dc22   2005007131
The paper used in this book meets the requirements of American
National Standard for Information Sciences—Permanence of
Paper for Printed Library Materials, ANSI z.39.48-1984. Binding
materials were selected for strength and durability.

University of Nevada Press Paperback Edition, 2007
16 15 14 13 12 11 10 09 08 07   5 4 3 2 1

ISBN-13: 978-0-87417-727-5 (pbk. : alk. paper)

Frontispiece: Robert Beckmann © 2001.
Detail of City Planner (After Poussin).

CONTENTS

ACKNOWLEDGMENTS

Margaret Dalrymple, former editor in chief at the University of Nevada Press, first encouraged me to write a book about Las Vegas, an enthusiasm continued by Joanne O'Hare, who was her successor and is now the director of the press.

I started researching the essays for *In the Desert of Desire* while a visiting scholar at the Getty Research Institute during spring 2002. Charles Salas, the director of the program, was kind enough to keep me on as a reader in the library throughout the duration. During the writing of the book I was fortunate to have a fellowship from the John Simon Guggenheim Memorial Foundation and a semester as a Hilliard Fund visiting scholar at the University of Nevada, Reno. My thanks to Bob Blesse at the UNR library for being such a fine host. Thanks are due as well to Scott Slovic, Cheryll Glotfelty, and Michael Cohen in the English Department, thinkers and writers who continue to inspire me.

I could not have written *In the Desert of Desire* without the help of numerous people in Las Vegas, most notably Phil Hagen and Scott Dickensheets. The former editor of *Las Vegas Life* and the editor of *Las Vegas Weekly*, respectively, Phil and Scott have provided me with a reason and budget to write about the city in the variety of guises over the course of several years. I first wrote about the Rio art collection, water issues, and the Las Vegas Springs Preserve for the former publication.

Other Las Vegans who have provided me with invaluable insights over the years include but are by no means limited to: Lee Cagley, Patrick Gaffey, Robin and Danny Greenspun, Polly Hahn, Dave Hickey, Nancy and Kell Houssels, Jim and Joy Lane, Bill Lowman, Libby Lumpkin, Steve Molasky, Hal Rothman, Jerry Schefcik, Mark Tratos, Roger Thomas, and Art Wolfe. The many artists, arts administrators, and people working in both public and private conservation efforts in and around Las Vegas have my thanks for twenty-five years of conversation and friendship.

As always, my work is vastly improved by the work of conscientious editors, and never more so than by the incomparable Gerry Anders, whose insights and encyclopedic knowledge corrected errors of fact and grammar. Please note, however, that I can attribute none of my opinions expressed herein to those people or authors whose works I quote in the text, and the responsibility for any mistakes resides solely with me.

PREFACE

This is a book about the presentation of art, animals, and sex in American society as seen through that very peculiar filter, the Las Vegas Strip. In particular, it's about how Las Vegas has uniquely blurred the roles of for-profit and not-for-profit entities in the exhibition of those three attractions. The first time I noticed this phenomenon was when driving down the Strip one midnight in 1986, and there was a Jenny Holzer *Truism* up on the Caesars Palace marquee: "Protect me from what I want." The New York artist's aphorism loomed overhead, her bright letters illuminating alike the tourists and the prostitutes.

The message, clearly a critique of the temptations offered on the Strip, was sponsored by the Nevada Institute for Contemporary Art, a nonprofit organization funded with state and federal public funds. Yet it was being displayed by a for-profit casino (or "gaming resort," as management would have it) as an advertisement. The largest single chunk of revenues in the Nevada treasury comes from the Las Vegas casinos—so the profit at Caesars Palace was paying for a message critical of the business, and the owners were donating the space to show it. What was being sold, I wondered?

The anomalies continued to pile up: The Strip literally turned its back on the desert, exclosing it behind a wall of hotels in order to protect the fantasy of the street, but the owners then re-created fake desert environments inside the hotels and populated them with exotic animals from Africa. The lions and tigers and elephants on the Strip put to shame the efforts of the local nonprofit zoo to attract locals, much less tourists. And then there was the lure of sex, the promise of which was only thinly veiled in the very nearly nude dance revues in the showrooms. And how did the dancers themselves relax after work? By forming a nonprofit ballet company funded jointly by the casinos and the state arts council.

During the 1980s and '90s, while I was watching all this happen in Las Vegas, the city became the fastest-growing metropolitan area in America. At the same time, the legalization of gambling spread across the country, in part in reaction to budgetary shortfalls at the local and state levels in places as varied as Wisconsin, Illinois, and Mississippi. The table and slot-machine games pioneered in Las Vegas started cropping up on riverboats and in Indian casinos. The practice of "theming" service and retail businesses, an art of simulation based in large part upon Hollywood's influence, had been perfected in Las Vegas from the 1940s onward. Now it was spreading from the resorts into everything from chain restaurants to housing developments. But influences were flowing in the other direction, too. Picasso and Matisse joined Jenny Holzer on the Strip.

And all along I kept wondering: What's being sold? *In the Desert of Desire* is an attempt to answer that.

～～ I've been working in and writing about Las Vegas since 1979 and have come to consider it a strange attractor in our culture. Like a magnetic pole, it pulls in and organizes inchoate desire into patterns of behavior that are bizarre but compelling to contemplate. The rules underlying the patterns are tax laws, both the federal ones governing the operation of nonprofit arts organizations and the more libertarian Nevada statutes that privilege the hotel-casinos over local governments.

The book started out as a meditation on the nature of culture in Las Vegas but almost immediately encompassed the culture of nature, in part because of the arc I've been following in my other books. For the last decade I've been writing about ways in which human cognition interacts with land and transforms it into landscape, and nowhere is that process demonstrated more vividly than in Las Vegas. Deserts, by virtue of their great open spaces and relatively thin stratigraphy of culture, allow us to observe the interaction of humans with the environment more easily than in temperate regions, which are more densely vegetated and settled. As a species we're not well equipped to function in the desert. We lose our sense of physical scale and perspective in such landscapes, which opens a gap between what we think we are seeing and the reality. And the Strip exploits that gap as far as our imaginations will allow.

The greater the dissonance between perception and reality, the more extreme our cultural responses become in order to compensate. The Mojave Desert is one of the most arid places on the planet, and Las Vegas therefore a correspondingly strong presence in it. Between the open field of view presented us by the desert and the exaggerated gestures we make in response to its foreign nature, we are provided an unparalleled opportunity to examine social behavior. That local culture responds to and is thus shaped directly by its immediate physical environment, as well as by the momentum of history and national identity, is not a new argument. Neither is the obvious corollary: that local cultures inform and influence national character. But the synergies are stronger in Las Vegas than in most other American cities, and they are more visible. Las Vegas is an intense locus of financial activity in the middle of one of the world's most severe deserts. Like its predecessors, ranging from ancient Babylon to Luxor, and its contemporary counterparts—Baghdad and Riyadh, for example—it is able to capitalize upon that fact by allowing people to imagine and then erect castles on the sand and into the air. Given the application of sufficient wealth, desert societies have few constraints in the short term, not even water. Deserts offer unhindered space in which to build and few objective correlatives—such as trees, buildings, and other attributes of more temperate environments—in nature or culture to constrain style. As a result, desert cities often present us with spectacles unimaginable elsewhere. The legendary Hanging Gardens of Babylon are a classic example, as is Caesars Palace. You simply don't find such extravaganzas in New York City or Minneapolis. And when you see a themed resort in Atlantic City or Miami, you've found a business inspired by the Las Vegas Strip, the most aggressively branded and promoted concatenation of adult theme parks in the world.

Just as great wealth allows humans to overrule for a time the local environmental conditions, so it can alter the sociopolitical ground rules. The Mojave Desert, by virtue of appearing to us as a blank slate, encourages us to erect buildings that abandon convention—but it also isolates Las Vegas from some of the political conventions that hold sway over other parts of the country. Steve Wynn, who has built the most opulent resorts in Las Vegas, spent more than half a billion dollars on art during the past ten years and was able, as one of Nevada's most powerful businessmen, to persuade the Nevada legislature to provide him with various forms of tax relief for his purchases, treating him in essence as if he were a nonprofit art museum. Most Nevadans don't mind at all that a casino owner has turned inside out the separation of powers between the for-profit and nonprofit worlds, a barrier that people in other states hold tantamount to the separation of church and state.

The future of Las Vegas depends upon its collective ability to fantasize our desires while balancing population growth with the availability of space and water. It isn't enough to survive in the desert by building the world's most visited tourist attraction, which since 1999 has outdrawn the annual pilgrimage to Mecca; Las Vegas must also constantly reinvent itself as our desires shift ground in relationship to other entertainments. Indian casinos, immersive role-playing computer games and gambling on the Internet, the file-sharing of music and movies . . . what Las Vegas has done, successfully for the most part, during the last fifty years is to outdistance such distractions and to cater directly to our desire to experience immortality. And that is what I think is being sold—the oldest and most desirable commodity known to humankind.

Las Vegas maintains its allure by continually refreshing the illusion that we are in the presence of immortality. It is able to do so because it is a highly creative place in terms of both creating artifice and manipulating organizational structures at a large scale for the presentation of the illusion. Hence, Steve Wynn changing tax laws.

In the Desert of Desire is both a critique and celebration of how Las Vegas creates spectacle in response to our desires. In writing about how vast sums of money flowing through Las Vegas have warped local social forces—a gravitational field that elsewhere maintains more widely separated orbits between for-profit businesses, nonprofit organizations, and government—I've chosen as my case studies the presentation of art and architecture, menageries and zoos, and dance and sex. Those are the arenas where we can witness the blurring of distinctions as they are on public display. Because gaming and the theming of businesses have proceeded outward from Las Vegas, I believe that the local anomalies have both metaphorical resonance and social implications for the rest of the country.

Art museums, zoos, dance companies—all have deep roots in multiple cultures, but all emerged as the nonprofit organizations we recognize today during the nineteenth century. The history of nonprofits, a particularly American institution, is closely related to our desire to keep government out of our philanthropy, a libertarian viewpoint that collides head-on with the need for public amenities in Las Vegas. What might be a public undertaking in another city, such as an art museum or an aquarium, becomes an attraction in a hotel-casino here. But at the same time, museums and zoological attractions around the country are creating profit centers as public funding becomes insufficient to maintain them. Nowhere else is the cross-dressing of nature and cultural presenters more evident than in Las Vegas.

Because I'm concentrating on subjects that are at the extreme ends of the curve, I'm not writing about the majority of local arts and nature organizations in Las Vegas. At the outset, therefore, it's important to state that Las Vegas is home to thousands of artists and performers, many with regional and national reputations. Nonprofit arts organizations have flourished here for decades, and various departments within the University of Nevada, Las Vegas (UNLV) have produced significant practitioners in all the artistic disciplines. Likewise, a number of local environmental groups are active in helping to preserve the surrounding desert, promote water conservation, and save archeological resources—but they are not the topic of discussion here.

～ Before offering my observations, some disclosure is in order. I lived in Nevada for thirty-three years, and worked in a casino after college for five of them while running a small nonprofit publishing house. I then served as assistant director at the art museum in Reno before taking a job at the Nevada Arts Council, where I stayed from 1980 to 1993. During the late 1980s I worked on national arts-policy issues and simultaneously was the co-owner of a bi-state for-profit outdoor retail corporation. When I left Nevada, I continued to work as a consultant to a variety of state arts agencies, private foundations, and nonprofit arts organizations. During the last twenty-five years, I've spent the equivalent of four of them in Las Vegas.

I've seen nonprofit arts organizations in town grub for money at the feet of the most unsavory corporations imaginable, fueled sometimes by greed and personal aggrandizement but more often by a shortage of funds and consequent fear of losing the ability to serve the community. I've watched local private corporations act generously toward artists and nature organizations, more often than not to improve their image or bottom line but sometimes simply because enlightened leaders sought to promote the local culture and to improve the standard of living for as many Las Vegans as possible. And I've seen state and federal government act in partnership with all of them, sometimes for better, sometimes for worse, but often with unpredictable results.

If it sounds as if my personal experiences have led me to disavow absolutes and to embrace a spectrum of behaviors and motivations among the three sectors of the American economy, then I've successfully communicated my bias to you. But then, the desert encourages flexibility as a survival strategy.

And finally, a word of caution. Narrative scholarship is, in essence, a report from the field. Although it may provide a valuable and even entertaining firsthand analysis of a subject, mixed with scholarly research, it has significant limitations. It is anchored in a specific time and place, and things change. Las Vegas morphs more quickly than any other city on the planet, and some of the particulars described here will have been altered radically by the time you read this. An afterword at the end of the book will give you an idea of what I mean and perhaps offer additional insight into the ongoing nature of the changes and the dynamics underlying them.

IN THE DESERT OF DESIRE

1

EDIFICE COMPLEX

The border between California and Nevada makes itself apparent ten miles before you cross it. When you drive around the last curve on Interstate 15 before descending from the eponymously named Mountain Pass and into the Ivanpah Valley, several enormous structures appear at the far end of the playa, a lakebed that since the Pleistocene ended almost ten thousand years ago has been more dry than wet. Three hotel-casinos, a discount mall, and a nearby 500-megawatt, gas-fired, water-cooled power plant flank the freeway, forming a surreal gateway into the state, one that declares, "Abandon reality, all ye who enter here." The allusion to Dante's *Inferno* is strengthened not only by the feverish temperatures of the Mojave Desert but also by the sight of the Desperado roller-coaster on the left at Buffalo Bill's. It's actually a "hyper-coaster" that is one of the tallest and fastest in the world. Its cars drop 215 feet and hit 95 miles per hour at the bottom, which in my book is considerably more like torture than entertainment. Las

Vegas is still thirty-five miles to the north, but the address out here is 31900 Las Vegas Boulevard South. Only a range of hills, another arid valley, and 319 blocks to go.

The high-rise hotels of Primm rise out of the Mojave with nothing to buffer them from the floor of the scorched alkali flat. No trees, houses, strip malls. It looks like a set for a cheap cowboy movie, the Wild West architectural touches on Whiskey Pete's and Buffalo Bill's not even trying to echo a real western town so much as a cartoon one. The layers of resemblance are not coincidental.

To drive from Los Angeles to Las Vegas on Interstate 15 is to inject yourself into a financial circulatory system that extends up the pseudopod of civilization from Hollywood's Sunset Strip to Las Vegas Boulevard, a growth that metastasized during the middle of the twentieth century. Los Angeles began to boom during the first two decades of the last century in one of those closed feedback loops destined to breed environmental malignancy. Oil was discovered in several fields around the L.A. Basin in 1892. In order to get workers to the fields, a network of far-flung roads was built, which of course meant an increasing number of cars, which in turn depended upon the petroleum being pumped out of the ground, which was an incentive to explore for more oil, which meant yet more roads.

This local synergy, emblematic of what would become an international one, produced a style of living centered around the automobile, and the image of a mobile society was woven deeply into the American psyche by the fact that Hollywood became the movie capital of the world just as the population of automobile drivers exploded in Los Angeles County. The mythos of the movie star and the automobile were fused from the beginning, and among the conjoined pleasures were motels, which in the 1930s along the original strip — Sunset Boulevard — were known as "motor hotels."

I-15 goes east through the L.A. Basin and then swings up the Cajon Pass around the northern end of the San Bernardino Mountains. If you go east on I-10 around the southern end of the range over the San Gorgonio Pass, you end up in Palm Springs, which on a day of light traffic takes less than three hours to reach from Hollywood. At first this proximity was a convenience for the movie stars and producers looking for a weekend retreat where they could escape the gossip columnists—then it became a liability. The motels of Palm Springs weren't quite far enough away to deter what would in later decades become known as *paparazzi*. Las Vegas, however, was. Furthermore, in order to get there you had to cross the Mojave Desert, an experience guaranteed, by virtue of the cognitive dissonance suffered along the way, to liberate your senses. Driving to Las Vegas—a task that, before the advent of automobile air conditioning, was best accomplished during the night—was a disorienting experience, and thus one quickly romanticized as an adventure into the exotic.

Hunter S. Thompson put it this way in his hallucinogenic romp *Fear and Loathing in Las Vegas:* "We were somewhere around Barstow on the edge of the desert when the drugs began to take hold. I remember saying something like 'I feel a bit lightheaded; maybe you should drive . . . ' And suddenly there was a terrible roar all around us and the sky was full of what looked like huge bats, all swooping and screeching and diving around the car, which was going about a hundred miles an hour with the top down to Las Vegas. And a voice screaming: 'Holy Jesus! What are these goddam animals?'" The reader's mileage may vary from Thompson's, but drugs only enhance what havoc the desert wreaks upon our mental balance; once you get sixty miles out of L.A. and into the high desert, your senses are loosened from reality. The Los Angeles cultural critic Ralph Rugoff, writing about the relationship between the desert and Las Vegas, said in *Circus Americanus* that the Mojave "supplies a prophylactic barrier against reality." Deprived of familiar plants and much in the way of buildings, we lose our sense of scale in the desert. The air is so clear that we mistake mountains twenty miles away to be within easy hiking distance of the car, should we choose to stop. And because the air is so dry, perspiration wicks off our bodies before we can feel it, so we don't even realize how hot it is. Our mind thinks it understands what it is seeing, but it doesn't, and after a while that visual dissonance becomes obvious—when, say, the other side of the valley you're driving through, which looked to be only five minutes away, turns out to be a half hour's drive at sixty-five miles per hour.

Out in the desert there's little to contradict our expectations, and architectural fantasy blooms in the American Southwest as naturally alongside the road as do the astonishingly large and white blossoms of the poisonous datura plant, which is held sacred by Native Americans for its ability to generate visions when properly prepared and ingested. The early motels along the Sunset Strip sometimes featured a modicum of themed decor, often derived from popular cowboy movies or the more sybaritic *Arabian Nights*. Both motifs made their way to Palm Springs and then to Las Vegas, the same architects being hired to design the lodgings in all three locations. The open desert was a hothouse for what would become a luxuriant architectural garden.

The first hotel on the Las Vegas Strip—the street that begins more than three hundred blocks to my north—was the El Rancho. It was built in 1941 by Thomas Hull alongside Highway 91, the original road from Los Angeles paved just a few years earlier. Hull, who owned eight traditional hotels in California, had recently begun constructing luxury motor hotels, all of them named El Rancho, the one in Las Vegas being his third. It immediately attracted the attention of movie stars who were looking for a new place in which to let down their hair. The next year, the movie-theater magnate R. E. Griffith opened the Last Frontier in Las Vegas and used his contacts to bring in Hollywood entertainers. Judy Garland was married in the wedding chapel on the premises, and Howard Hughes began his lifelong association with the city as a guest at the hotel.

Benjamin "Bugsy" Siegel is usually credited with ushering in the Las Vegas age of spectacle with the Flamingo, a relatively sumptuous resort that opened in 1946 at a cost of what for the time was an astonishing $6 million. The price of construction was so over the top, in fact, and the operating deficits so large (caused in part by his skimming) that the mob had him bumped off at his house in Beverly Hills. But Siegel was building on a foundation laid, literally, by Billy Wilkerson, who owned a nightclub in Hollywood and was one of the founders of the *Hollywood Reporter*. Wilkerson had run out of money, and Siegel, a handsome mobster who was also a wannabe actor, moved in. Siegel's assassination only increased the allure of Las Vegas for people in the movie industry. Within months the Desert Inn, which would exceed the price tag of the Flamingo by another half million, was under construction; during the 1950s it established an early standard for touristic luxury that Las Vegas resort owners would still be cultivating four decades later.

Jay Sarno took the next step. Born in 1922 and a teenager during the depression, by 1958 he was building what he called Cabana motor hotels in Atlanta, Palo Alto, and Dallas. The Cabanas' landscaping and interior decoration relied heavily on fountains, statues, and mirrors. When Sarno visited Las Vegas in the early 1960s, he assessed the state of its amenities as being still less than ideal and persuaded his friend Jimmy Hoffa to lend him $10.6 million in Teamsters Union pension funds to build Caesars Palace, the first genuinely themed establishment in town. The architectural details, which evoked ancient Rome, included yet more fountains and statues, exotic touches that audiences had been prepared to recognize by movies such as *Ben Hur* (1959) and *Spartacus* (1960). Even the employees wore costumes designed by a wardrobe mistress. Sarno's idea was that every visitor should be made to feel like a Caesar or a Cleopatra, not just a walk-through on a stage set—hence the lack of an apostrophe in the name, lest a customer be reminded that, in fact, the resort was not his very own residence. The logo, logically enough, featured a scantily attired woman dripping grapes into the mouth of a toga-clad citizen, an obviously phallic dagger hanging naked and fully extended from his side.

Although Sarno had himself gone to Italy to photograph architectural details that he could appropriate, the theming wasn't simply a matter of facade and graphic kitsch, but the creation of a three-dimensional experience with walking and talking centurions, cocktail waitresses in abbreviated versions of Roman dress, and a level of luxury elevated to rival that of a schoolboy's dream of imperial Rome. When the fourteen-story, seven-hundred-room hotel opened in 1966 the construction bill totaled $24 million (with an additional million spent on the opening night party). High rollers lolled about on Cleopatra's Barge, which floated in an indoor pool and rocked sensuously to the swaying steps of the waitresses, who in fact peeled grapes for the patrons. The place was a smashing success, and Sarno escaped the fate of Siegel (or, for that matter, Mr. Hoffa). Everyone marveled at the spectacle that was Caesars, and the Strip would never be the same.

After Sarno, the ante was upped by the insatiably acquisitive Kirk Kerkorian, who had first become involved in Las Vegas through running charter air flights from L.A. Kerkorian supersized the hotel business, first opening the International (now the Las Vegas Hilton) in 1968 with 1,512 rooms. In 1969 he gained stock control of the MGM Corporation, which gave him access to an entertainment empire. His second megaresort, the MGM Grand (now Bally's), opened in 1973 with 2,084 rooms. In 1993 he launched a new MGM Grand, built at a cost of $1 billion, with 5,009 rooms and its own amusement park. Each was the world's largest hotel when it opened.

The building progression on the Strip from the El Rancho to the second MGM Grand was one of increasingly large properties that relied on a growing synergy with Hollywood, using by association the glamour of the movie industry to make the exoticism of Las Vegas—some of it *faux*, some of it genuine—attractive to the national audience of a mass medium. Movies such as *Ocean's Eleven* (both the 1960 Rat Pack original and the George Clooney–Brad Pitt–Julia Roberts remake shot at the Bellagio in 2001) and *Viva Las Vegas* (the 1964 musical starring Elvis Presley and Ann-Margret) helped create the image of Sin City as a place highly luxurious and mildly dangerous, a seductive combination that television has continued in shows featuring private detectives and criminal investigators in the city, notably *Vega$* (1978–1981) and the current high-tech *CSI: Crime Scene Investigation*. Increasing the size of the properties kept costs down so that middle-class Americans could afford the experiences for themselves, as if they had stepped through the screens of the movie theaters and television sets and onto a sound stage for the Roman Colosseum, if not into the arena itself.

Steve Wynn was a careful student of what his predecessors had wrought. He openly admired Sarno's use of water and statuary at Caesars, and he obviously paid attention to the economy of scale deployed by Kerkorian. Wynn, who has never strayed far from the business principles he learned at the University of Pennsylvania's Wharton School, not only was entrepreneurial in spirit but also based his moves on research, which in later years would include the use of focus groups and an internal polling operation. His instincts and research both guided him to provide his customers hotels without neon, casinos where women felt as comfortable as men, and an unparalleled variety of upscale recreational and retail amenities.

Siegel had used entertainment mostly as a way to distract customers from dwelling upon their losses at the table; Wynn realized that more people shop than gamble. Furthermore, he knew full well that the glamour of Hollywood was itself a *glamour* in the original sense of that old Scots word—a magical (in this case theatrical) spell cast on the public—and that contemporary Americans were sophisticated enough to be intrigued by the real thing. There was money to be made—and greater glamour to be accumulated—by providing not merely the illusion of richness through props but actual treasures to be purchased. The gaming revenue in Clark County totaled $7.6 billion in 2002—but that year gaming accounted for only 43 percent of the revenue at the Mirage. Las Vegas as of 2004 has more than 130,000 hotel rooms, having added 60,000 of those along the Strip during the 1990s alone. The average room rate is around $100 a night, and occupancy overflows on the weekends to other towns such as Laughlin—and Primm. The financing of the Bellagio was predicated on not only bringing people to the tables but also luring them to upscale shops, restaurants, and Cirque du Soleil's extravaganza *O*, an aquatic circus show that cost $110 per person to attend.

～～ Leaving Primm in my rearview mirror, the two casinos reversed left to right, I think about how the Italian writer Umberto Eco used both the Getty Villa in Los Angeles and the Las Vegas Strip as examples of the "absolute fake" in the title essay of his seminal book *Travels in Hyperreality*, written in the early 1970s.

The essay initiated an ongoing discussion about the nature of imitation in American architecture and society, a debate over our desire to achieve immortality through art. The openings, in 1997 and 1998, respectively, of the most expensive museum in the world, the new Getty Center, which vastly expands the mission of the Villa, and the most expensive hotel-casino in the world, the Bellagio in Las Vegas, present an irresistible provocation to continue comparing the two into the twenty-first century. There is more than a passing similarity between the themed environments of the Getty and the Italianate hotel-casinos of the Strip, a useful *frisson* when writing about the nature of culture and the culture of nature in Las Vegas.

A milestone in the history of national cultural spectacle was the opening of Steve Wynn's Bellagio Gallery of Fine Art in 1998. Featuring $300 million worth of paintings by masters safely entrenched within the canon of nineteenth- and twentieth-century European and American art, the presentation of such a collection in a casino toppled the already crumbling wall between what were once considered high and low cultures by Las Vegans.

Wynn's Bellagio Resort was the single most expensive building in the world when it opened—a thirty-six-story luxury hotel that included an underground parking garage for six thousand cars, a convention center, and an enormous gambling floor. The resort's interior space totaled 6 million square feet and was fronted by a $52 million, ten-acre, 22-million-gallon lake in which a fountain with 1,200 jets shot water 250 feet into the air, the streams synchronized to dance along with classical music, which was broadcast onto Las Vegas Boulevard via loudspeakers as well as piped into the hotel rooms. The Bellagio cost more than $1.6 billion to build, a figure touted by local tourism officials as proof that Las Vegas was invincible as a destination. To place art into such a context intrigued the resort industry, interested to see if the experiment would generate profit, either directly or indirectly. The gallery brought cautious approval from local cultural leaders, who hoped that Wynn was leading a charge to overthrow the image of the town as a cultural wasteland (which in reality it has never been).

The Getty Center, which had opened only a few months earlier, is a 24-acre campus that includes a museum, research institute and library, and four other principal buildings, all nestled within a 750-acre parcel on the southern slopes of the chaparral-covered Santa Monica Mountains. The complex, much of which was set underground in order to address neighborhood concerns about height restrictions, put a total of 1.6 million square feet under cover and took fourteen years to design and build. It cost approximately $1.3 billion, a scandalous amount in the art world when it opened in 1997. Travertine panels covering 1.2 million square feet were brought from the same Italian quarry that supplied the stone for the Roman Colosseum and the colonnade of Saint Peter's Basilica; 40,000 enameled metal panels and almost 165,000 square feet of glass completed the exterior. Where the Bellagio planned for a high volume of traffic, having discovered through focus groups that tourists like to gawk at overt displays of wealth, the Getty seriously underestimated the novelty of the world's most expensive museum, and provided only 1,200 spaces in its garage.

Although the Bellagio was envisioned to stimulate visceral excitement, and the Getty to encourage contemplation, the public saw both as accessible spectacles exemplifying wealth, which is to say reality writ large via artifice. The Getty during its first year was drawing up to 10,000 people a day, which overwhelmed both the parking facilities and the reservation system. The Bellagio drew 80,000 people in its first eighteen hours of operation, and the art gallery itself was pulling in 1,800 daily at $12 per head (versus the free admission to the Getty). Parking at the casino was seldom at a shortage, but the long lines to see the paintings surprised Wynn and everyone else.

Critics derided the new Getty Museum as the overblown manifestation of an edifice complex, as if they were embarrassed that anyone in the art world would spend so much money on a facility, proposing that instead the Getty administration should have put a higher priority on buying art. I find this logic somewhat peculiar, as if you would counsel someone to buy fine antique furniture and then build a tract house in which to put it. The resort industry, initially skeptical of the budget for the Bellagio, turned smartly on its heel when it saw the first month's gaming take and saluted Wynn for his visionary accomplishment. The art critics, a tougher crowd, remained skeptical of the Getty's price tag.

The designers of the Bellagio, Jerde Partnership International, are known for their experiential designs combining themed architecture, retail space, restaurants, and entertainment into synergistic environments that encourage people to spend money. Universal CityWalk, which opened in 1993 in the Hollywood Hills, is a prime example. It anthologizes Los Angeles along a two-block pedestrian promenade that replicates in miniature everything from the signs on Sunset Strip to the beach at Malibu, the latter complete with machine-generated waves, thus offering the public an animatronic version of nature and culture as an entertainment in which to go shopping. Jerde likewise designed the Bellagio to create a sense of place akin to that of the town of the same name on Lake Como in northern Italy, though a hint of Monte Carlo is deliberately invoked at the same time. The public, instead of vacationing in the Mojave Desert, would be tourists in Italy, a much more exotic locale that offered exclusive opportunities to spend money at European boutiques. Wynn, in fact, had created an elaborate

backstory for his resort in order to flesh out its theme: The ficti-
tious Count and Countess of Bellagio, made wealthy by their international banking and hotel interests, create an estate in Las Vegas,
where the count can rest easier with his asthma. As the family fortunes decline and the grounds fall into disrepair, Wynn purchases
the property and converts it into his resort, its fabulous treasures
now rescued and made available to everyone.

Richard Meier, the architect of the Getty, who is known for his
rigorous organization of stone, glass, and metal panels into tight
rectilinear grids, was also following an architectural model derived
from the Old World. Because the Getty imposes an orderly geomet-
ric vocabulary upon a hillside, it has been compared to the Acropo-
lis above Athens and to Hadrian's Villa outside Rome. Both are
elevated sites, the former dominated by the hypnotically regular
columns of the Parthenon, the latter counterpoising extensive gardens and reflecting pools to the emperor's art collection and offering carefully constructed vistas over the surrounding countryside.
The modernist vocabulary developed during the twentieth century
by Le Corbusier (1887–1965) and Mies van der Rohe (1886–1969)
and subsequently expanded by Meier (born in 1934), has roots
deep in that Greco-Roman heritage. The modular concrete forms
used by Le Corbusier were scaled to the human body as were the
columns of the Parthenon, and the regularity of glass draped over
steel by Mies van der Rohe evoked the mathematical sense of order
prized by both the Greeks and the Romans. That visitors ride an
electric tramway three-quarters of a mile each morning to reach
the Getty, up a hillside planted in a neoclassical grid of oak and
other trees, only enhances the feeling of entering a kingdom as
magical as that of any other theme park.

The Bellagio and the Getty shared speciality designers, which
reinforces the comparison. Claire Tuttle works for Water Entertainment Technology, a firm that has created water features for

Disney and Universal CityWalk in Los Angeles, as well as the fountains in front of the Bellagio. She took a leave of absence in order
to help Meier design the exterior running water at the Getty. The
international firm Wendelighting illuminated galleries at both the
Getty and the Bellagio, in each case observing the necessities of
conservation while creating distinctively luminous environments
for the art.

You can push the architectural comparisons only so far, however. Where Jerde is overtly appropriating classical design in order
to create a simulacrum of the original—a fake that is patently a
fake and thus real on its own terms—Meier is creating new forms
to concatenate with old ones and enlarging a tradition. The Bellagio is the calculated representation of a place, the Getty Center
an original distillate of one. The hotel-casino refers to the exotic
of the faraway, while the Getty's rectilinear stones and aluminum
panels are a cartographic allusion to its own locale, the Los Angeles
grid spread out below.

Likewise, you can compare Steve Wynn to Jean Paul Getty only
to a certain extent, but it is nonetheless an enlightening exercise.
Getty was born in 1892 and followed his father into the oil business. He was a millionaire by the 1930s; when the tycoon died
in 1976, he was a billionaire and one of the richest people in the
world. He started collecting art seriously in 1931 and was spurred
in his efforts by the example of his next-door neighbor on Malibu
Beach, the media magnate William Randolph Hearst, at whose San
Simeon estate Getty spent New Year's in 1934 as a guest. The newspaper magnate's 90,000-square-foot pastiche in concrete of a
lavish and improbable southern Spanish castle awed Getty, and he
would eventually seek to outdo it, though on his own more conser-
vative terms. In 1945 he built a ranch house in Malibu and in 1953
opened a small museum of antiquities in a wing built for that purpose. He moved to England soon thereafter, in part for purposes

of easing his tax burden, and settled into a large sixteenth-century Tudor estate, Sutton Place. Instead of importing a European fantasy to America, he exported himself into the reality.

Getty continued to acquire art and antiquities and in 1974 opened a small Roman-style museum on the Pacific Palisades hillside above the beach. Whereas Hearst commingled authentic and imitation artworks with Italian, Spanish, Egyptian, and Gothic architecture at his castle, seeking to fulfill his own desire to collect all of civilization, Getty adhered scrupulously to archeological plans in order to re-create the first-century AD Villa dei Papiri near Herculaneum. It was modeled in concrete and beautifully detailed but could showcase only part of his extensive collection. Getty was never to visit his own museum, no doubt discouraged in part by published comments that excoriated the lack of consistent quality in his holdings and by some critics' comparisons of the villa to a Disney attraction. The author Joan Didion, an acute observer of her native California, noted in 1977 that the somewhat out-of-the-way $17-million building was so swamped by visitors that it could be visited by appointment only. She surmised that although the critics decry wealth, the public is fascinated by it.

In addition, Getty had his own notions about the value and exhibition of fine art. Although he cared enough for the paintings he owned to spend years, in some cases, researching their individual provenance, he also justified his selections for purchase by how well they fit into the various styles of rooms in his houses. Needless to say, such a decorative basis for collecting was visibly at odds with the rhetoric of museum curators, who sternly value artworks for their supposedly discrete and intrinsic value as aesthetic objects—although how one is supposed to separate the formation of value from a society rooted in consumerism remains somewhat of a conundrum.

Getty had always been blunt that furniture and rugs, which is to say objects at least nominally utilitarian, could be great works of art on a par with paintings and sculpture, and he stated in the manner of his time that he could assess a man's financial worth by what he put under his feet. At one point he unrolled one of the world's greatest works in fiber, the sixteenth-century Ardabil Carpet, on the floor of his penthouse apartment in Manhattan. The priceless 23.5-by-13-foot Persian carpet, woven in silk and wool with 15.5 million knots total, may have taken six artists as long as four years to weave and now resides at the Los Angeles County Museum of Art. Getty valued it for its beauty, the amount of work that went into its creation, and how it looked on his floor, using more than one definition for what constituted a work of art, and more than monetary or historical measures by which to assess its worth.

The stated mission of the Getty Museum, which follows the dictates of Getty's will, is "to delight, inspire, and educate a diverse public through the collection, preservation, exhibition and interpretation of works of art of the highest quality." It and the other institutes on the hill are funded by the Getty Trust, which received $1.2 billion upon Getty's death and after the claims of the heirs were settled; the amount almost doubled when the Getty Oil stock was sold in 1984. During the stock market bubble of the mid-1990s, the principal grew to more than $5 billion. These spectacular increases forced the trust to spend enormous amounts of money within a relatively short time so as not to violate federal tax laws, which specify that such nonprofit entities must expend at least 4.25 percent of their endowments in three out of every four years. The enormous expenditures of the trust are encouraged, therefore, by tax law, though the corpus was temporarily much reduced by the bursting of the dot.com bubble.

Steve Wynn, like Getty, followed his father into business. The elder Wynn was himself a gambler who visited Las Vegas with his ten-year-old son in 1952 and for a short while ran a bingo parlor there before returning east. The younger Wynn eventually attended the University of Pennsylvania. When his father died, Steve took over his bingo business in New York. In 1967 he returned to Las Vegas with his wife, Elaine, and bought into the Frontier Hotel. After engaging in a variety of business ventures, by 1984 he was already worth $100 million. In 1989 he opened the Mirage, the first new major hotel built on the Strip since 1973. The three-thousand-room resort cost $630 million, and the junk bonds sold by his friend Michael Milken to finance the construction carried a such a high debt load that the property needed to make more than $1 million a day to service it. Although Milken didn't suffer Hoffa's fate as a financier of casino construction, that same year he was indicted by a federal grand jury for violation of securities and racketeering laws. He pled guilty to lesser charges, received a two-year prison sentence, and was required to pay the govern-ment $42 million in fines. Nonetheless, the first hotel-casino on the Strip not to use neon on its facade and signs flourished, and Wynn moved on to build the much more expensive Bellagio, which required an estimated $2.7 million daily in gross receipts to be profitable.

Getty made his first notable art purchase in 1931, a landscape by Jan van Goyen bought at an auction in Berlin for $1,100. In 1996 the Getty Museum's art and archival acquisitions budget, accord-ing to Kurt Anderson writing in the *New Yorker*, was $110 million. In 1990 van Gogh's *Irises*, at the time the most expensive painting in the world, had been bought by the Getty for an undisclosed sum reported to be between $30 million and $65 million. (Its previ-ous price at auction—in 1987 to the Australian businessman Alan Bond, who proved to be unable to pay for it—was $49 million.) Wynn started buying art for the Bellagio collection in 1996 and in that first year paid $3.4 million for Modigliani's 1916 portrait of the art dealer Paul Guillaume. Within two years he had spent approximately $300 million on the art collection, $75 million of which was his own money. Ever since, he has been a major driving force in the international art market, which in 2003 saw approximately $2.3 billion in auction transactions. Getty has been called an indifferent collector, and the museum has worked hard to rectify shortcomings in the collection. Wynn has been voracious in his purchases from the beginning, and agents for both the Getty Museum and the resort developer were present at the same auctions of impressionist and Old Master works during the 1990s. In fact, Wynn bought a Seurat in 1999 for $35.2 million that the *Los Angeles Times* art critic Christopher Knight castigated the Getty for not purchasing. That same year Wynn paid $60.5 million for a Cézanne still life of fruit.

Wynn's fine-art purchases were also a prudent strategy for dealing with federal tax laws. They transferred capital into assets that continued to accrue monetary value as well as social status. By displaying them to the public while retaining the right to sell them, Wynn gained a measure of tax relief, as had Getty. Unfortunately, Wynn was forced to sell off Mirage Properties in 2000, due in no small part to his shareholders becoming nervous about such lavish use of corporate funds to buy art. Kirk Kerkorian/MGM Grand bought Mirage Properties for $4.4 billion in cash, as well as assuming $2 billion in debt. Those artworks owned by the Bellagio were sold off to help retire around $150 million of that debt. Wynn was left with just over a dozen pieces belonging to his personal collection.

〜 What I mean to set in motion by piling all these facts and figures next to one another is a comparative inquiry into how we value culture and nature in our society, an examination made possible by the fact that the enormous amounts of money spent in Las Vegas warp, and in some cases simply demolish, the walls between private pleasure and public consumption. There are connections among the exhibition of art, lions and tigers, and the dancers in Las Vegas, all of which relate to the worship of exoticism, the creation of social status, and the codification of moral values via aesthetics in politics. And all of it is centered around the desire to place ourselves near immortality.

IN THE GALLERIES

My first stop in Las Vegas is a reconnaissance of the Bellagio (3600 Las Vegas Boulevard South, thank you very much). The art gallery is closed for a few days while the staff installs an Andy Warhol show. I'll attend the opening later in the week, but I want to start by looking at the spectacle of the lobby, and I talk the local painter Robert Beckmann into meeting me. Beckmann has lived in Las Vegas since 1977, when he moved here under the aegis of the state arts council to work as an artist in the schools, a program funded by the National Endowment for the Arts. In those early days of the program, the most popular projects undertaken by the artists-in-residence were usually murals for schools, designed and then executed in collaboration with the students. It was a way of involving as many kids as possible, of enlivening the drab cement block walls of institutional architecture, and of leaving behind a semi-permanent reminder that the government was funding arts education, even as school districts were being forced by budget cuts to eliminate art teachers from classrooms across America.

The increasingly tight federal and state education budgets of the 1980s squeezed out many school art programs, including artists residencies, but by that time Beckmann was an established muralist in Las Vegas, and commissioned by a number of public and private entities to commit art on walls. His mural business continues today to support his studio art, some of which is also bought by casino executives and their interior designers to be placed in the resorts, a crossover that is not uncommon in town. Thousands of artists have worked in the casinos to help create—or re-create—the statues, paintings, and *objets d'art* that patrons expect when venturing inside casinos whose overarching theme is luxury, no matter if the setting is Rome, Venice, or Lake Como.

We start our tour of the Bellagio with the Dale Chihuly ceiling in the main lobby. Neither Beckmann nor I is a fan of the artist's work, though we admire the technical facility it takes to create the largest glass sculptures in the world. Chihuly blew his first glass in 1965 and then earned his master of fine arts degree from the Rhode Island School of Design. While a young artist he worked more in avant-garde installations—making enormous statements in glass, neon, and dry ice—than as a craftsperson per se. But in 1969 he received a grant to become the first American to study at the famous glassworks in Murano, Italy, outside Venice, and during the 1970s he began making more object-oriented art (versus utilitarian vessels), such as his series of glass cylinders inspired by Navajo blankets. In 1980 he created his most widely recognized style, large glass objects colored with metal oxides, hand-blown, and spun by centrifugal force into softly fluted shapes that resemble undersea flora. The ceiling eighteen feet above us is thick with the extravagant glass flowers.

Beckmann shakes his head in dismay. "Look at how it's so layered that complementary colors—orange and purple, or red and green—actually overlap and become muddy."

It's a well-known story that each time Steve Wynn came in to inspect the sculpture, titled *Fiori di Como*, he would gaze up at the ceiling, remark that he could still see white space between the large glass pieces, and ask that the artist create enough additional work to eliminate the blank spots. Most artists prefer a little white space around their objects in order to set them off from the rest of the world, allowing the mind to engage more fully with them, and Chihuly is no exception; but Wynn, whose vision suffers from the degenerative disease retinitis pigmentosa, was adamant. Chihuly had originally designed the "chandelier" to consist of approximately a thousand pieces floating within the seventy-by-thirty-foot soffit. By the time he was finished with it, five tons of steel were required to float the twenty-ton combined weight of 2,164 overlapping individual pieces, all of which cost Wynn a reported $10 million.

I have no idea how Chihuly felt about his client's aesthetics, but the painful irony of Wynn's being legally blind is often noted by local artists. The disease has severely narrowed the avid collector's vision over the years, reducing the pleasure that he can obtain from paintings down to that partaken through a magnifying glass focused on only one small part of a canvas at a time. People often speculate as to how Wynn's malady may influence his demand for visual intensity in his environments, but the larger issue is one of the need for spectacle in Las Vegas. And spectacle translates into visitors' being visually stunned, in this case not by an imitation of art but by an original artwork.

The first time I met John Frohnmayer, then the newly sworn-in chairman of the National Endowment for the Arts, was when I picked him up at Las Vegas's McCarran International Airport at midnight one evening in 1989 and delivered him to the Mirage, where he was staying for a conference. John was a bit bleary, it being three in the morning his time, and it was gratifying to see him come thoroughly awake when, as he was registering, he looked up and into the fifty-three-foot-long saltwater aquarium behind the front desk. It wasn't so much the sight of a full-grown shark swimming by that got his adrenaline going, as it was the janitor in a scuba outfit following close behind with a net in hand as he performed the nightly cleanup.

The Mirage had opened earlier that year, and its hourly volcanic eruptions out front, rainforest atrium and aquarium inside, plus dolphins and white tigers out back had already made it the most popular tourist attraction in Nevada, outstripping even Hoover Dam. According to Chihuly, when Wynn asked him to design the *Fiori di Como* piece for the Bellagio, he wanted something "spectacular" that would rival the aquarium at the Mirage. Chihuly's forty-thousand-pound upside-down seafloor must have seemed just the ticket.

Visual spectacle is also what the garden adjacent to the Bellagio's lobby has to offer. Its flowers, like the shark in the tank next door, are real. At this time of year the theme of the conservatory is Chinese New Year's, and thousands of strange orange fruits are impaled on wooden pikes scattered among the flowers. A stuffed white mountain goat is mounted on a pedestal to celebrate the Year of the Ram, and hundreds of Asian tourists crowd the aisles taking pictures and capturing video. When the resort first opened, Wynn engaged Martha Stewart to design the first Christmas in the conservatory, and the monthly changes of the floral arrangements cost $8 million annually.

At the far end of the overwhelming floral barrage is the Chihuly Gallery, a bit of profitable synergy for artist and patron. The showroom is an alarmingly tight five hundred square feet or so, and one is forced to swivel one's shoulders carefully when turning about, lest one inadvertently mow down several thousand dollars' worth of large glass flowers. The polite young lady inside informs me that the prices range from $1,000 to $40,000.

There's another reason, besides providing an air of luxury, for the intense patterning found in casinos — be it the dazzling floral patterns of the carpets or the madcap faces of electronic slot machines. As the art critic Barbara Rose points out in her essay on Chihuly's projects, our reaction to his work is not to transcend them but to "drown in them," to become "lost and physically disoriented" or "rapturous" and "ecstatic." Not only does that kind of density increase our feelings of being pampered in some exotic pleasure dome, but it also helps us lose track of any objective correlative to our experience. Reality is swamped, and we lose track of time and space, a cognitive dissonance created not through the austerity found in the desert outside, but through its opulent opposite. No clocks, no windows, just mirrors, endlessly circling aisles, and cocktail waitresses — all the better to encourage you to stay at the tables, unconscious of the hours. In the lobby on our way out, I look up and envision Hunter S. Thompson tilting his head back at the Chihuly ceiling and being rooted to his spot for an entire night.

⌇ Later in the week I visit the Bellagio Gallery during a press preview of its exhibit of celebrity portraits by Andy Warhol. The gallery, located at the opposite end of the resort — meaning you have to traverse the gaming floor in order to reach it from the front desk — used to be an almost overly exquisite environment in which to view art. Walls covered in a forest-green mohair provided a deep contrast to the artworks, which were lit with framing lights that covered the images but did not spill outside the individual frames. The result was that the paintings were illuminated as if they were precious jewels, an effect calculated to raise the visitor's instinctual estimation of their value.

The gallery closed temporarily in late May of 2000 when Kirk Kerkorian bought Mirage Resorts, but in the nineteen and a half months it was first open, 630,000 people visited it—roughly 33,000 people per month, sometimes standing in line for up to three hours to view what were, in actuality, genuinely important paintings in the history of Western art, with price tags to match. Today, hotel guests stroll by the gallery, glancing curiously at the glossy black press folders stacked neatly on a table by the entrance. A young woman from one of the better public relations firms in town checks me in, then walks me through a velvet rope queue to the entrance, at the same time offering me an interview with the chairman of the gallery, Marc Glimcher.

I first visited the gallery when it still housed Wynn's collection. The two rooms, totaling a modest 2,600 square feet, held thirty-six paintings by artists such as Matisse, Pissaro, and van Gogh, including *The Head of John the Baptist Presented to Salome* as painted by Rubens in the early 1600s, an important and stunning work that one could only hope would eventually land in a museum. The dense fabric that was then on the walls has since given way to bare Sheetrock—painted almost black for the Warhol exhibition—and the richly patterned casino carpeting has vanished in favor of polished wood planks.

The more than fifty Warhol paintings and silk-screened prints, starting with a 1960 collage of James Dean, are based on images from publicity stills, newspaper photos, and shots taken by Warhol with an inexpensive handheld Polaroid camera. A dozen or so people with notebooks and pens wander from picture to picture, some holding audio wands to their ears, listening to Liza Minelli reminisce about the artist and his subjects. Her ad lib comments are a bit arch in spots, but also well informed about how Warhol's work plays within the history of both art and Hollywood celebrities. The exhibition concludes in a small narrow room with a time-line of the artist's life, a case containing his Polaroid camera, and his trademark silvery wig, which a stylist has just refurbished and placed on its stand.

Most of the works in the show have been lent by José Mugrabi, who according to Judd Tully writing in *Art + Auction* is an Israeli-born Colombian textile trader and internationally known art spec-ulator who owns what is reputed to be the largest private holding of Warhol paintings in the world. The collector, who packages his holdings into exhibitions for rent, is himself strolling about the gal-lery in a lightweight suit with a leopard-print scarf wound around his neck and a designer clutch tucked under his arm. He beams at Marc Glimcher, gestures with his free arm, and proclaims himself happy "to be among my people." Glimcher smiles back, an affable man dressed in a dark suit. A few minutes later we manage to have a short conversation about the show and PaperBall, the company that now packages exhibitions for the hotel.

After MGM disposed of the artworks formerly owned by the resort as part of the effort to pay off some of the Bellagio's stag-gering debt load, the gallery reopened in September of 1998 with a selection of paintings from the Phillips Collection in Washington, DC. In what was then an unusual arrangement, the Bellagio didn't rent the show but split the proceeds with the Phillips. The exhibi-tion lasted six months, and the Phillips claimed to have pulled in $1 million from the 150,000 people who walked in the door. Fol-lowing that, the Los Angeles actor, author, and art collector Steve Martin lent twenty-eight works from his private collection, which, although it included pieces by Seurat and Picasso, consisted mostly of contemporary American art. The proceeds went to the Steve Martin Charitable Foundation, a private organization that funds the arts. Martin, a well-educated collector who also sits on the board of trustees for the Los Angeles County Museum of Art, narrated the audio guide, the script for which was written by the *New Yorker* art critic Adam Gopnik.

The Bellagio found, however, that running what was becoming a small exhibition hall was beyond their administrative abilities. After unexpectedly losing negotiations for the next show, it gladly let out operation of the space in a long-term lease to Paper-Ball, a subsidiary of one of the nation's largest dealers in modern and contemporary art, the PaceWildenstein Gallery in New York. PaceWildenstein was founded by Marc's father, Arnold "Arne" Glimcher, in 1960, while Arne was still a junior at Boston University working on his bachelor of fine arts degree. Since then he has handled works by artists from early-twentieth-century modernism, including Henry Moore and Picasso, the midcentury giants Agnes Martin and Donald Judd, and current blue-chip stars such as Chuck Close and Elizabeth Murray. At the same address is Pace Prints (which sells, among other things, prints published by Pace Editions), which was started concurrently by one of Arne's closest friends, Dick Solomon. Marc tells me that there's no contractual or corporate marriage between PaceWildenstein and Pace Editions but acknowledges that an obvious beneficial relationship exists. If the New York gallery is showing some of the immense portraits painted in oil by Chuck Close and the publisher is issuing an edition of prints by the same artist, sales of the two reinforce each other by reaching complementary market niches.

Not only was PaperBall able to respond in a few weeks to the Bellagio's needs with an Alexander Calder show, The Art of Invention, but the gallery's gift shop sold tens of thousands of dollars' worth of related merchandise, including expensive limited-edition prints. PaceWildenstein was showing off its merchandise; Pace Editions and Pace Prints had just found a new venue. The next exhibit was Fabergé: Treasures from the Kremlin, which Marc tells me attracted 140,000 visitors during the months it was up, more than any other gallery show — anywhere by anyone — that he could think of.

Pace in all its permutations is not exactly a transparent business. The value of contemporary artworks depends a great deal on art dealers' careful management of speculation, rumor, and a deliberately opaque synergy among galleries, museums, publishers, and media. PaperBall is a rare example of how such networks can morph into a codified and relatively public manifestation. According to Marc, Andrea Bundonis — who has a degree in art history, was formerly the director of public relations for Pace, and will soon become his wife — proposed to Pace that they start a subsidiary devoted to exhibition services. By putting together shows of work by their clients — be they the estates of individual artists such as Calder or those of collectors — and offering them to galleries and museums, they would be offering the public access to artworks that might otherwise remain unseen. More important, they would also be raising the value of said works by lengthening their exhibition pedigrees, collecting reviews, and creating demand among buyers. Among PaperBall's first assignments was quickly mounting an exhibition for the Bellagio's empty gallery.

"Will you ever use this space as a selling gallery?" I ask Marc.

"No," he replies emphatically. "That would kill the gallery permanently. What we're selling here is an art experience." He pauses. "Not, mind you, that we can afford to lose money. We're not like the Guggenheim, which could afford to lose money; we have to earn our way."

Well, not exactly. The Guggenheim Las Vegas exhibition facility across the street spent $30 million just to stay open for only a year, and a couple of weeks ago closed the doors on the larger of its two spaces in town. But I get his point: Pace and PaperBall are for-profit entities working without the safety net of public subsidy or private donations. And Mugrabi? On top of the rental fee he collects for the show, he's also being paid part of the gate. Tully will later report in his magazine profile of the collector that 125,000 people paid $15 to see the Warhol exhibit. Although none of the fifty Warhol works will be sold directly out of the Bellagio, Mugrabi, like Wynn, frequently sells works from his collection, and the exposure here raises their value in the marketplace.

Glimcher excuses himself by simply letting the conversation wind down, and I wander off to make a final round of the portraits. Beckmann, when I told him I was coming to the press preview, was mildly derisive. He likes Warhol's work to a point but in general finds it to be more about surface than depth, more about fame than substance. But as the art critic David Hickey points out, Warhol was known for getting things "exactly wrong"—and showing a selection of the artist's work curated around the theme of celebrity is a fine example of that principle still in action.

Warhol, born to Czech immigrants in Pittsburgh in 1928, grew up as the definitive outsider in his family. Talented, gay, and with cheekbones preternaturally hollowed out by a desire to be rich and famous, Warhol attended the Carnegie Institute of Technology and in 1949 earned a degree in pictorial design. He moved to New York, where he published illustrations in such prominent fashion magazines as *Vogue* and *Harper's Bazaar*, but by 1952 he had his first solo gallery show in the city, fifteen drawings based on the writings of Truman Capote. His earliest silk-screened celebrity piece was a 1962 portrait of the actor Troy Donahue based on a publicity still, and for the next two and a half decades he painted and silk-screened images of pop icons from Marilyn Monroe to Mao Tse-Tung, Elizabeth Taylor to Michael Jackson. Among the artistic products coming from Warhol's Factory, as his cavernous studio was called, was wallpaper. He went from creating posters of famous people to becoming one himself, the household synonym for pop art.

Warhol is a fine choice to exhibit at the Bellagio because he understood the nature of spectacle—the complicated overlayering of materials and images until they overwhelm the senses, creating the giddy numbness that we associate with rich chocolate and gold bullion. On my left as I begin my last walk-through is a series, lent by Dick Solomon and his wife, of Marilyn Monroe faces printed in hallucinogenic tones. It's so bright and repetitive that I can hardly bear to look at it, which is itself a comment on the sexual attraction Monroe offered the culture. Then there is one of the few black-and-white pieces in the show, and my favorite, *The Men in Her Life*. The image, taken from a newspaper photo, shows Elizabeth Taylor with her then-husband, the Hollywood producer Mike Todd. Beside them are the singer Eddie Fisher and his wife, the actress Debbie Reynolds. The picture was taken in 1957, and by 1959 Todd was dead, killed in a plane crash, and Fisher had divorced Reynolds. Nine months later he married Taylor. Warhol, when he printed the silk-screen in 1962, repeated the image thirty-some-odd times, a comment on the claustrophobic social inbreeding of the movie world. He referred to it as "celebrity wallpaper." It's exactly the wrong thing to say about people, much less about a close friend, as Elizabeth Taylor was to Warhol. And yet it also captures how we dehumanize celebrities by fetishizing them, a process the mass media abet by overexposing their images in print and on television. So it's exactly right.

Looking at the silk-screen, which is nearly the size of a wall in my apartment, I'm reminded of the two large Robert Rauschenberg prints, commissioned by Wynn and completed in 1999, that flank the long front desk in the hotel lobby. *Lucky Dream*, on the left, features found images such as a trophy, Asian cranes and tigers, and the Sistine Chapel. It's about luck, obliquely refers to the role that high rollers from Hong Kong play in the financial well-being of the casino, and inadvertently provides an art-historical matrix for the Chihuly ceiling. *Overnighter*, at the other end, offers a similarly dense collage of elements from popular culture. People checking in ignore them as if they were, indeed, just more wallpaper. If Beckmann is correct about Warhol's dealing with the surface of things, then Warhol may be the perfect artist for Las Vegas, a city constantly erecting ever more elaborate facades that asymptotically approach the genuine.

〜 Later that day I drive up the Strip, having once again corralled Beckmann into joining me. We pass the Bellagio and head north to see the art gallery at Wynn's new resort, Wynn Las Vegas, under construction on the former site of the Desert Inn. Originally named Le Rêve, or "The Dream," after the Picasso painting of the same title that's now owned by Wynn and his wife, the resort received its new designation after focus groups proved to Wynn that his own name was far more recognizable than an obscure French phrase. The timing of the change—when American restaurants were renaming french fries "freedom fries" in retaliation for the French government's refusal to lend support to our invasion of Iraq—was a bit coincidental for my taste. At first I was put off by Wynn's use of his name—until I remembered how many museums in America are named for their founders. Whether it's the Getty, the Guggenheim, or the Wynn, the operant principle is branding, and use of a person's family name remains the single most common way to establish a strong identification in a consumerist society. Offering your family moniker on the sign out front is a public act that we unconsciously accept as a guarantee of authenticity.

Wynn Las Vegas is being billed as the most opulent resort in Las

Vegas and, at something around $2.4 billion to build, is currently the second most expensive construction project in the world (after the Big Dig in Boston). Totaling five million square feet, it will have more than double the floor space of the Empire State Building, and its fifty-story, 2,700-room hotel tower will be the tallest in Las Vegas. Along with Ferrari and Maserati dealerships, and the only eighteen-hole golf course on the Strip, it will have a new water-themed show produced by the former director of Cirque du Soleil, Franco Dragone. And, of course, the hotel will also have Steve Wynn's new art gallery.

All of this has resonant parallels with the history of the Desert Inn, known locally as the "D.I.," and the classiest joint in town until Wynn came along. The D.I. was built by a former craps dealer from Reno, Wilbur Clark, who started construction in 1946. Within two years he was so far over budget that he was forced to accept an offer from the noted mob figure Moe Dalitz, who ended up owning 74 percent of the two-hundred-acre, $6.5-million property. The hotel was built of cinder blocks but trimmed with sandstone and finished throughout the inside with redwood. It had three hundred rooms, was run by a former manager of the Clift Hotel in San Francisco, and was the first in town to feature a fountain out front. The latter included a show of "Dancing Waters" with the jets choreographed to music. The hotel's Sky Room restaurant once hosted the highest vantage point on the Strip, and the chef had worked at the Ritz Hotel in Paris. The D.I. was the first and only resort on the Strip to offer an eighteen-hole golf course, which Wynn has now inherited.

The Desert Inn went on to become one of the most venerable properties in town. Frank Sinatra had his debut there in 1950, Noël Coward performed for a month in its showroom, and Howard Hughes liked it so much that, after being threatened with eviction from its top floors in 1966 by incoming high rollers, he simply bought the place. He lived there until he died in 1976, at which point Kirk Kerkorian bought it. After Wynn sold Mirage Resorts to the MGM, he turned around and bought the D.I. for $270 million—the largest piece of property on the Strip with lavish water rights.

The echoes between the D.I. and the Wynn are numerous, obvious, and deliberate, even in the use of art. The Painted Desert Room, the D.I.'s restaurant and showroom, had themed murals by an honest-to-god immigrant French artist. Charles Cobelle, born in Alsace-Lorraine in 1902, emigrated to the United States in the 1920s and established himself as both a studio and a mural artist. Although his work never gained wide respect in the museum world, it is still promoted by dealers in art posters as belonging to the French "open line" school, in his hands a bright and almost naive style that used bold black lines to outline forms that were then washed in color. The technique lent itself well to illustration and was often adopted by midcentury graphic artists, especially those theming imitation Parisian cafes.

At the Wynn Las Vegas construction site, structural steel for the hotel is in the ground, dwarfing the one remaining piece of the old D.I., a ten-story tower that now contains offices and the temporary art gallery. A lone gentleman manning both the gift shop and the gallery door admits us, and we find ourselves once again in a jewelbox setting with tightly focused lights illuminating each of the dozen or so paintings. Matisse, van Gogh, Cézanne, Manet, Modigliani, Picasso, Warhol—it's much the same cast of characters originally featured on the marquee outside the Bellagio, and now appearing on the multistory sign out front here.

Beckmann pokes his nose so close to the Matisse, a late (1940) still life titled *Pineapple and Anemones*, that the security alarm goes off. The very quiet guard standing in one corner approaches and taps him on the arm. This is a recurrent problem with Beckmann.

The first time I witnessed it was at the Getty when he thrust his thick glasses within an inch of *Landscape with a Calm* by Poussin and proceeded to give me a lecture on the artist's use of foliage. A guard was by our side within seconds, letting us know that he'd been eavesdropping on our conversation, presumably via a microphone mounted to the wall behind the painting, a security device often deployed in larger museums.

Beckmann was sufficiently rebuked to maintain his distance afterward at the Getty, but it says something about the intimate darkness of Wynn's gallery that he continues inadvertently to breach the low railing set on the floor in front of the paintings. When he sets off the alarm for the third time, the guard just waves at him from across the room. A museum would eject us, but this is a private establishment where no one knows exactly who you might be and everything is for sale. We wander from painting to painting, the only visitors in the gallery, a remarkable occurrence in a society where these works in a museum almost anywhere else would draw a constant stream of viewers. It's a reminder that art in the resorts is a just another attraction for most people, and without other experiences to be had in the same building—slot machines, white tigers, four-star restaurants, erupting volcanoes—hardly anyone will bother to drive a few blocks for the sake of a Manet.

〜 Back outside, the bright sunshine and noise are painful after the dim hush of the gallery. The late afternoon traffic is beginning to build on the Strip, and although crews across the wide boulevard have stopped construction for the day on the expansion of the Fashion Show Mall, a high-end shopping destination, workers labor noisily on Wynn's property 24/7—erecting rebar during the day and pouring cement during the night. An elevated crosswalk will link Wynn's resort with the mall, giving his guests immediate access to Neiman Marcus and hundreds of other stores. On the far side of Wynn's parcel sits the Las Vegas Convention Center, and I can't even begin to estimate the foot traffic that will circulate among the three facilities. Shopping is now a more popular pastime among the 35 million people visiting Las Vegas annually than gaming, a trend reflected in casino revenues on the Strip, where less than 50 percent comes from gambling; the majority is earned by the restaurants, shops, and entertainments.

Wynn has a way of recognizing and capitalizing, literally, upon synergies, a word that I am becoming tired of using. It describes perfectly, however, that upward-spiraling concatenation of energies once known in certain business circles as "working the angles." Wynn's installation of a gallery first at the Bellagio, and now here, recognized not only that cultural tourism was the fastest-growing segment of the industry during the 1990s—and that more people attend arts events than sports events—but also that there was also a very profitable tax angle to be worked. In 1997, the year after he started spending what would, by the time of this writing, amount to more than half a billion dollars on art, he pushed through the state legislature a law that reduced the sales tax on paintings valued at more than $25,000 (and thus classed officially as "masterpieces") from 7.25 percent to 2 percent and exempted them entirely from the state's 1 percent personal property tax. So far the tax relief he has obtained is estimated in the tens of millions of dollars. Furthermore, after subsequent negotiation with the legislature, he was allowed to charge a $12 admission fee at his gallery, as long as he provided Nevada residents with a half-price ticket and let in schoolchildren free for sixty days per year. On top of these financial boons, he charged Mirage Resorts $5.5 million annually to rent his portion of the collection that it didn't own.

According to the "Art Rental and Licensing Agreement" between Wynn and Wynn Resorts that took effect on November 1, 2001, the new resort started paying him $1 million monthly on rental fees for the paintings, plus all of the adjusted gross (all revenues from admissions, retails sales, merchandising agreements, etc. after expenses). Furthermore, the resort pays insurance and property and sales taxes, as long as he adheres to the public viewing provisions.

So Wynn buys the art and is exempt from the tax for owning it. He leases it to the hotel, which earns more than enough in admissions to pay for the operating costs of the gallery. When he sells the art, he's exempt from most of the sales tax, although he is still subject to the capital gains tax if it has appreciated in value. And, like real estate, there are only so many square yards of masterpieces in the world, so the value mostly goes up, not down. (Wynn's leverage with the local tax assessor's office in Clark County is also powerful. Records from that office in 2003 show that the Wynn Las Vegas land on the Strip was valued at $27 per square foot, but comparable vacant footage belonging to the Mirage was assessed at $45–$51, and $47 for the Venetian.)

Nothing about the taxation of Wynn's art is illegal or even improper, although it's certainly inventive. In fact, it follows in the honorable American tradition of alleviating tax burdens by donating funds and goods to nonprofit, tax-exempt cultural institutions, which at the same time provides a demonstrable public benefit. The fact that Wynn Las Vegas is a for-profit venture is not as large a stumbling block for a legislated tax benefit as you might think. The Metropolitan Museum of Art in New York operates the most extensive museum store chain in the world; its eighteen branches in the United States, eleven in Europe and Asia, and its online business generate upwards of $74 million annually. And yes, the Met store has a branch in the Venetian hotel-casino down the street—where the Guggenheim Museum of Art also operates a branch in collaboration with Russia's State Hermitage Museum.

The blurring of the three sectors of the American economy—
for-profit, not-for-profit, and governmental—is constant, and
museums have been selling merchandise in this country ever since
the Met put up etchings for sale in 1871. Now more than eighteen
hundred museum stores exist in the United States, some generating up to a third of their host institution's annual operating budget. Even the Getty, rich as it is, pays close attention to its retail
operation, which in addition to its main store includes three satel-
lite shops located near the galleries featuring changing exhibitions
and was projected to earn $5 million in its first year of operation,
generating a profit of 20 percent. Museum stores as a whole do even
better than those at upscale regional malls. While a retailer across
the street in the Fashion Show might be expected to generate $200
to $300 per square foot and the very exclusive shops at the Forum
in Caesars Palace bring in $1,200 to $1,300, art museum stores can
rake in as much as $2,000 per square foot—and not pay taxes on
the earnings, as long as the merchandise is business-related.

As government funding for the arts declined in real dollars during the last two decades, museums turned increasingly to earned
revenues, of which store sales constitute the largest percentage.
During the 1990s gallery space at the nation's largest museums
increased by just over 3 percent, while space devoted to their stores
grew by almost ten times that amount. Consultants to the country's
1.6 million nonprofits have increasingly urged them to create retail
businesses. Zoos, aquariums, health organizations, churches, and
universities soon followed the example of the museums.

On the other hand, Saks Fifth Avenue gets designers to create
special clothes, then donates a portion of their sales to the Save the
Music Foundation, a nonprofit set up by MTV's video music channel VH1 to "restore music education programs in public schools,"
which were traditionally a publicly funded part of the curricula in

most American schools. The arrangement not only earns goodwill in the community for the retailer but also increases foot traffic in the stores.

This evolution of the relationships among for-profit and not-for-profit businesses as they display art appears to be more distorted in Las Vegas than in other cities because of the source and amounts of the money involved, the number and nature of visitors, and the relatively thin social veils in place. We expect to find showgirls in a casino, not paintings of ballerinas by Degas, which in theory should be isolated in a museum setting and free from commercial implication. In the context of Nevada history, however, it makes perfect sense that gambling pays for culture and the audiences are broader than your typical museum crowd dressed in black. The residents of Virginia City during the 1860s—a boomtown where wagers and fortunes were made and lost on the location of silver ore—would have taken the situation for granted. The miners offered lucrative contracts to lure internationally renowned actors and opera stars on their way to San Francisco to perform first at the local Piper's Opera House, and for a time the music scene in the notoriously rough mining camp rivaled that of any major city on the West Coast.

It's a long way in space and time from the dusty boardwalks of Virginia City to Las Vegas Boulevard, but when you drive down the Strip with the enormous neon signs are flickering on all around, it's obvious that both places were based on desire and on taking chances with the desert to fulfill it.

3

FAKING THE MUSEUM

A tradition for both tourists and visiting artists—groups sometimes pigeonholed by journalists as the ultrasquare and the
ultrahip—is to make the trek over to the Liberace Museum, the
largest building in a strip mall on East Tropicana Avenue near
UNLV (which used to house its graduate art-student painting
studios in the space). Liberace, an iconic Las Vegas performer,
received grants and scholarships for his entire seventeen years
in musical training starting when he was seven in his hometown
of Milwaukee, and later in life he became determined to repay the
favor. In 1976 he established a foundation that continues after his
death to fund millions of dollars in performing-arts scholarships
and to run the museum, a facility that exhibits everything from
his enormous rings to a mirrored Rolls Royce, as well as eighteen
of his thirty-nine pianos. The collection is a monument to the
recontextualization of gay culture in America through the safe
haven provided by Las Vegas.

When Wynn opened his gallery at the Bellagio, blasé tourists wandered in and inquired of the guards whether the art was authentic. After all, the biggest "gemstone" at the Liberace Museum is a 115,000-carat, 50.6-pound piece of lead glass, the world's largest rhinestone. Which is to say that, while you might not have expected to find fine art on the Strip during the last quarter of the twentieth century, flamboyant imitation was a given. No one would think to question the architectural authenticity of the New York Stock Exchange on the main floor of the New York–New York hotel-casino—it's patently a simulacrum, which is exactly the point. Of course, that didn't stop the real NYSE from suing New York–New York for trademark infringement when the resort reproduced the facade at a much-reduced scale, a suit that the court dismissed. Perhaps the board of the exchange forgot that their original 1903 building in New York is a reflection of the imposing neoclassical financial institutions in London (the Royal Exchange dates from 1842), which in turn are based just as obviously on Greek and Roman temples as is Caesars Palace.

When Sheldon Adelson opened the Venetian in 1999 after three years of intense fast-track design and construction interrupted periodically by financing difficulties and labor disputes, he had spent $1.5 billion. The Venetian, the Strip's first all-suite hotel, rose on the former site of the Sands, the hotel-casino that was the home of Sinatra and the Rat Pack. Adelson had proposed to replace Hollywood's favorite Las Vegas watering hole with a resort of incomparable sophistication, and he followed the lead of New York–New York and Paris with another city-themed project. The resort's three thousand suites rest atop an ornate eighty-foot-high podium, its three-story facade an elaborate collage of Venetian Renaissance architecture.

Inside are 1.5 million square feet of themed public space that include a three-hundred-foot-long Grand Canal, the Rialto Bridge, the Grand Hall in the Doge's Palace, and painted reproductions of frescoes by Titian, Tintoretto, and Veronese. In addition to numerous paintings framed in gold leaf and statues created by Adelman's team of 250 artists and art historians, "living statues" wander the retail spaces. On the ground floor Madame Tussauds opened its first U.S. wax museum. Among the more than one hundred figures in the attraction, Sinatra, Dean Martin, and Sammy Davis Jr. are displayed next to Presidents Washington, Lincoln, and Kennedy, while standing nearby are the likenesses of Bugsy Siegel and Liberace.

The layering of themed replication at the Venetian turned out to be the densest in town, the epitome of Las Vegas rococo — and therefore a highly charged context into which to interject the announcement that the Guggenheim Museum in New York would open two galleries inside the resort, one of which would be in collaboration with the State Hermitage Museum in St. Petersburg, Russia. The Guggenheim Las Vegas would be a 63,700-square-foot facility on two levels, and the Hermitage-Guggenheim a jewelbox at only 7,600 square feet. Both galleries would be designed by Rem Koolhaas, a postmodern architect known for his asymmetrical use of glass and steel. A more startling contrast with the tightly patterned symmetry of Venetian tilework could not be easily imagined, and the architecture critic Nikolai Ourossoff hailed the design in the *Los Angeles Times* as an act of courageous juxtaposition, a machine for showing art in the garden of earthly delights.

The galleries opened in the fall of 2000 and proved to be very successful in — well, if not exactly promoting the image of Las Vegas as a burgeoning center of contemporary culture that could accommodate highbrow as well as lowbrow attractions, at least in provoking a conversation about it in the national press, fashion magazines, and art journals. While the larger space exhibited The

Art of the Motorcycle, the smaller gallery hosted Masterpieces and Master Collectors, with forty-five paintings drawn from the permanent collections of the Guggenheim and Hermitage. According to Barbara Bloemink, then the head Guggenheim staff person in Las Vegas, the two galleries brought in 600,000 people the first year, 15 percent of whom had never visited an art museum before. (Visitor surveys disclosed that the newcomers had usually been too intimated by traditional museums to enter their doors.) Only 10 percent of the visitors were actually staying at the Venetian. Despite the imprimatur of the Guggenheim, Bloemink told me, some patrons still asked if the art was real.

Guggenheim Las Vegas was essentially a multilevel exposed-concrete box that Koolhaas designed to exhibit anything from Harley hogs to the steel "torqued ellipses" of Richard Serra. For the motorcycle show, the superstar L.A. architect Frank Gehry created a series of discrete spaces with swooping stainless steel ribbons. Gehry had recently finished the Guggenheim's museum in Bilbao, Spain, a building so successful that it drew tens of thousands of tourists to an otherwise economically depressed city, creating what critics hailed as the "Bilbao effect." The motorcycle show, curated by the Guggenheim Foundation's director, Thomas Krens, and partially sponsored by BMW, contained more than 130 motorcycles arranged in chronological order from an 1868 steam-powered Micheaux-Perreaux onward. When I walked through the exhibition, my feelings were similar to those of many other art writers: great motorcycles, cool if eccentric installation—and who, exactly, is the audience for this? I felt as if I'd wandered into a show at the National Automobile Museum in Reno. And what was it, again, that was being sold?

The Art of the Motorcycle first appeared at the Guggenheim in New York, and although everyone understood the connection between industrial design and art history, and the show drew the largest crowds in the history of the museum, it was criticized for two reasons. First, when Solomon R. Guggenheim established the museum in 1937, it was for the display of nonobjective art — nonrepresentational, abstract art of the twentieth century. It's a long stretch from the abstractions of Wassily Kandinsky, which celebrate the deliberate disconnection of paint on the canvas from representation of exterior reality, to the utilitarian engineering of a motorcycle, wherein the relationship of object to the world is manifestly designed to be between your legs.

The second criticism was based on a perceived conflict of interest in that BMW, a sponsor of the show, was also one of its primary subjects. Krens again created a similar controversy in 2002 when the museum mounted a large and well-attended exhibition of fashions by the designer Giorgio Armani. Armani didn't fund the exhibition directly, but the timing of a $15 million gift from the designer, announced only a month after the opening of the show, was unfortunate. Curation of objects by professionals implies that objective standards of judgment will be applied as to the value of the objects in the culture. The presence of money tends to distort the picture, so to speak.

Krens has both a master's degree in art from the State University of New York in Albany and an MBA from Yale, perhaps one reason he has not been as shy as some of his museum colleagues about making overt the links between art and commerce. His background prepared him to act when he visited Las Vegas and saw people lined up outside Wynn's Bellagio gallery. If such a small space could pull in two thousand people a day, what kind of traffic would a museum with a name like the Guggenheim's generate? The Venetian was an obvious choice for a theme, given the fact that an important part of the Guggenheim's collection of twentieth-century art resides in Peggy Guggenheim's palazzo on the Grand Canal in Venice itself.

~ The partnership that he formed with Sheldon Adelson was part of a larger Krens plan to brand the Guggenheim as the world's leading museum of contemporary art. Krens sought not only to deepen the Guggenheim's reach into art audiences worldwide by through new facilities everywhere from Las Vegas to Rio de Janeiro and Taiwan, but also to broaden the audience by bridging the gap between high and low cultures. That kind of two-pronged attack—deepening attendance by people who already like museums, while also reaching across to new demographics—is an ideal strategy in many respects but is also very, very expensive because it involves marketing outside one's obvious niche, which requires the use of mass media.

Although the two galleries came in on budget and met their costs, fund-raising and earned revenues at the parent Guggenheim Foundation in New York weren't doing so well after the dot .com bust, and then the events of September 11 trimmed attendance at the museums. The foundation's operating budget had fallen to half of what it had been in the late 1990s, and the board chairman would soon be forcing Krens into balancing the budget or looking for employment elsewhere. On top of the parent museum's troubles, the Venetian wasn't making much from the deal. Travel to Las Vegas dropped after the terrorist attacks, which negatively impacted tourism. The Guggenheim had predicted audiences of four thousand per day, but only a thousand or so were showing up. The larger gallery was closed only fifteen months after it opened and is now undergoing renovation for use as the resort's second showroom.

The smaller gallery, however, has gone on to mount small but handsome survey shows that continue to draw both critical appreciation and decent audiences, and once again I dragoon Robert Beckmann into accompanying me on a visit to yet another Las Vegas anthology of Western art's greatest hits, Art through the Ages: Masterpieces of Painting from Titian to Picasso. It's late October, and at valet parking a person with a professionally applied green face and crooked snotty nose gets out of the car in front of us, pulling on a pointed black hat. The valet instructs us to "follow the witch." Renaissance Italy didn't observe Halloween, but I suppose masked balls were common enough in Venice that our guide will fit into the decor.

～ The Venetian is organized around what has become the traditional division of resort spaces: games of chance on the first floor, entertainments on the second, and lodgings stacked in towers above. There are certain economies to be obtained in such a design. Because more people go shopping in the resorts than gamble there, make sure that customers coming in off the street have to wend their way through at least a corner of the gaming arena before taking the escalator up to the shops arrayed along the Grand Canal. If that means having to buttress and waterproof the second-story floor to hold a half million gallons (roughly two thousand tons) of water, the income generated will more than pay for the extra cost. What's interesting is that the two Guggenheim Museum gallery spaces were placed on the gaming floor, adjacent not to the retail entrances but to tables where people play games, thus putting art into the context of recreation rather than consumption, a not illogical choice.

The decor of the Venetian's lobby, located off a side-street entrance, is tastefully dressed down in black, cream, and various shades of brown—so the red poster advertising the Guggenheim gallery is a profoundly jarring note. At the top it quotes the *Washington Post:* "Sensationally sensual . . . showy, sexy, dynamic, dreamy," and at the bottom the *Los Angeles Times:* "Where entertainment is art, now art is entertainment."

Beckmann gets us both in as locals, thus obtaining a $3 discount from the general admission price of $15, and a woman punches our tickets at the automatic glass doors that, once they close behind us, eliminate completely the clamor of the slot machines. The smaller gallery has been renamed the Guggenheim-Hermitage Museum, a purely rhetorical ploy for public relations. It's a gallery, not a museum, as the original press release from Krens noted: the facility doesn't collect or curate art but was designed simply to exhibit it. But the public reacts more favorably to the notion of a museum than a gallery. The latter is taken to mean a place that both shows and sells art, as with Wynn's original Bellagio Gallery, and the Guggenheim is trying to distinguish itself from the commercial nature of Wynn's operation. The recent reversal of names from Hermitage-Guggenheim to Guggenheim-Hermitage has a more obscure rationale, stemming from the economic reality of who is now paying more money to rent the space from the hotel.

Rhetorical flourishes aside, the space is quietly spectacular. The gallery is a rectangle framed by Koolhaas in half-inch-thick Cor-Ten steel, a material revered by outdoor sculptors for its ability to rust only on the surface, thus maintaining its structural integrity while producing a soft, velvety texture. The enormous sheets here were allowed to oxidize into that mellow state and then waxed, resulting in a paradoxically warm leather look. The steel walls are suspended from structural columns, leaving a few inches of clearance between their edges and the floor, a gap filled with translucent glass. When you're outside, you can see the dim outlines of people's shoes, a sight that induces curiosity about, and even envy of, those inside. It's clear that the gallery is an exclosure creating a privileged space. What's being sold? Desire. Once inside, the brightness of the gallery precludes you from seeing out, reinforcing that notion of privilege, and the richly patinated walls seem to hover effortlessly in place.

Bloemink articulated to me some thoughts about surface in Las

Vegas after her job there had been eliminated in the downsizing: "The Strip is pure entertainment based on superficial surfaces, like a Hollywood set with nothing behind it. It's meant to have a fast, physical appeal that creates a rush, versus art, which is about very careful, extended viewing. The Strip is about surfaces that seduce you, whereas paintings are in and of themselves real objects that draw you underneath the surface into meaning. Art is about individual responses, the Strip about group dynamics."

Thirty-eight paintings are held to the walls by magnets, each and every work, from a small van Eyck to a large Jackson Pollock, shown behind glass. "It's that high-quality museum glass that hardly reflects anything," Beckmann observes through his coke-bottle glasses, "but still, it's unfortunate. It takes away all the surface and tactility." He presses his nose up to a painting, and I shudder, remembering our experience with guards at the Getty and the Wynn Collection. Beckmann might complain about presence of the glass, a condition the Hermitage insisted upon in the exhibition contract for works on loan, yet it allows him to go eyeball-to-eyeball with the reddened orb of Jesus carrying the cross as painted by Titian in the 1560s—and the guard ignores him.

Unlike Wynn's gallery at the Bellagio, where the works were pinpointed in spotlights, here the atmosphere is open and evenly lit, glare on the glass a potential problem that is magically almost nonexistent. We wander from the fifteenth-century van Eyck portrait of Jan de Leeuw, past a small Dürer portrait done ninety years later, and through the Renaissance. I'm pleased to find both Jan Steen's morality tale *In Luxury Beware* (shades of Jenny Holzer) and one of my favorite paintings by Claude Lorrain, *Morning in the Harbor.* Both are often reproduced in art history books, and it makes me grin to see the originals in Las Vegas. I catch my breath, though, when I spot Picasso's *Woman Ironing* across the room, a melancholy study from his Blue Period of a young woman pressing down on a shirt with both hands. It's a painting I've loved since I was fifteen, and I haven't seen it in years.

The crowd changes around us, people entering with their digitally recorded art-history lessons pressed to their ears, proceeding from one numbered painting to the next and then out the glass door at the other end and into the museum shop with its ties and cups and t-shirts. Beckmann and I circle among the three guards and thirty other patrons, making several rounds through all the paintings. We sit, we stand, we talk and gesture. We point and mumble to each other and ourselves, and I take notes on a small folded piece of paper. Our behavior is distinctly not that of the other patrons, and I'm acutely aware of the guards constantly shifting position to keep us in a direct line of sight. They may not care how close we get to the paintings, but our contravention of the normal circulation through the art catches their attention.

The art history that's presented in the gallery is summary but, if reductive, is also curated with intelligence, each painting illuminating the context of its neighbors. It's romantic stuff with a nice mix of names that many people will recognize and some that they won't. One young man, probably a painter, spends many minutes intently studying the flesh tones in a Velázquez. A couple of black-suited women from New York converse knowledgeably about Kandinsky's *Blue Mountain*. A young couple strolls in with their acoustic guides, obviously bewildered by it all.

Beckmann and I are the least decorous people in the place, talking out loud and being far too boisterous. There is a clear difference between this show and the Wynn galleries, and it makes us almost giddy with pleasure. Some of the paintings that Wynn has bought and put on display in his galleries are of a quality and significance on a par with the paintings here, but the context is utterly different. His space is a private gallery, the works assembled according to his individual taste. These rooms belong to two of the world's great encyclopedic museums, and the works are drawn from enormous vaults filled with objects selected by curators trained in art history. From such vast collections curators can assemble an almost infinite variety of narratives. Steve Wynn has only one short story to tell—that of his development as a collector and the increasing level of intelligence and focus he has brought to bear on that process. The museums' permanent collections are built from donations of many collectors through the years, as well as the institutions' own purchases. They can unroll novel after novel. Among these paintings Beckmann and I, even without the audio wands, can hear numerous voices murmuring tales in our ears.

～ The traditional function for museums as understood in our culture is to collect, preserve, and display objects from the past or present so that current and future generations can learn from them. That objective implies that the audience can decode the original references contained within the objects—as, for example, Renaissance churchgoers could read the messages promulgated by the stained-glass windows in a medieval cathedral (one reason that, in turn, museums are often compared to places of worship).

This object-oriented mission is based on continuity, but it is matched in contemporary times by a parallel mission, one based in change, whereby curators seek to shift the framework of understanding to convey new viewpoints and knowledge. The main method used in doing this is unexpected juxtaposition—putting one object next to another so that they can establish a dialogue, which is then often made overt through a wall text, acoustic guide, or docent lecture. You can discover continuity through time, or discontinuity. You can do the same with spatial relations, contrasting objects from the same time but from different countries.

Putting motorcycles or designer gowns in an art museum is one way of using juxtaposition to ask questions about the nature of culture itself—while, admittedly, seeking not only to broaden a society's notion of what constitutes art but also to raise some serious cash at the box office. Design is, after all, a set of aesthetic concerns that your average pragmatic American citizen is raised to understand, whether it's from reading *Vogue* or *Road & Track*.

What the insertion of the Guggenheim galleries into Las Vegas demonstrates, however, is something beyond simply the interjection of either motorcycles or Monet into the themed architecture of the Strip. The objects are no longer there to create a narrative that you read. The insertion foregrounds how the object in and of itself is less what is of value than is the experience of viewing the object—which is why the museums are near the slot machines, not the retail boutiques on the second floor. Both the art and the gambling are aspects of spectacle.

The Strip, once competition arrived in the form of gambling in other states and on Indian lands, morphed into mass spectacle. It became a pedestrian experience where people go to stroll the neon-lit sidewalks at night in order to participate in something larger than life, larger than themselves. You go to Las Vegas precisely because you want to be overwhelmed by an excessive visual ordeal. We define and describe spectacle by the use of superlatives, and Wynn tells you on his taped message that his paintings are the "most expensive" and "the best." The Guggenheim's advertising offers the viewer no less.

The Guggenheim, in putting art on the Strip, is not fulfilling a serious cultural mission any more than Steve Wynn's galleries are—though this is not to say that Krens and Wynn don't appreciate art. But as Wynn positions himself through tax laws closer to being a nonprofit art presenter and Krens maneuvers the Guggenheim toward providing profit-making spectacles, it's apparent that the ground is shifting. When a museum purchases a painting these days, it is not merely acquiring an object for study by and enlightenment of your grandchildren, it's also capturing an asset that will generate revenue through admission tickets, retail sales, image licensing, touring fees, and resale appreciation. The objects have no intrinsic value, by this measure, other than how they are experienced, and the more elaborate and expensive the presentation of that experience, the higher in value is the object held in the marketplace. This is not to say that artworks are simply commodities; quite the opposite. But they can be manipulated as if they were, and artists, dealers, and museums, via advertising and public relations, can and do manipulate them in this way.

The Guggenheim-Hermitage has an active educational program that brings thousands of schoolchildren into the exhibitions, and Wynn's gallery is obliged by statute to provide a similar service to the community. The museum also has experimented with a free-after-5 program for residents on Tuesday evenings. According to the Guggenheim-Hermitage's managing director, Elizabeth Herridge, 25 percent of the attendees during that Tuesday time slot are locals. That participation, she says, translates into "a couple of hundred people signing up for players cards," which the casino uses as a promotion for gambling. As Doug Humble, a friend of mine in Marfa, Texas, once commented, "In Las Vegas, it's the museums that are fake, not the paintings."

Despite Herridge's efforts, it would be easier for a museum in Las Vegas to perform a genuine cultural service that is active instead of passive, and is more about knowledge than about entertainment, if it were a locally grown, private, nonprofit, tax exempt, community educational institution. In short, it would have to be a real museum and not a mere exhibition space posing as one in order to increase the verisimilitude for tourists of walking in the presence of luxury.

4

BRANDING IMMORTALITY

On the far western edge of the city, housed in a library building, is an art museum ostensibly run for the benefit of Las Vegans. Like many other local and regional art museums birthed in
America during the post–World War II prosperity, the Las Vegas
Art Museum (LVAM) started out as an artists' collective. The Las
Vegas Art League was established in 1950 to provide an organization through which members could hold classes and the occa-
sional sales event. In 1966 the city purchased the property that
would become Lorenzi Park, and the league petitioned for and
was granted use of an old motel on the public premises, a shotgun
affair with a dubious history. They remodeled the dismal lineup
of rooms into a modest sales gallery and shop and began to collect
and store a few pieces of local art, mostly amateur works by league
members, even though the building offered no hope for the climate control and security a permanent collection should have.

In 1974 the group obtained nonprofit, tax-exempt status and

changed its name to that of a museum, which was still more of a promise than a fact. The LVAM's board of directors tried throughout the 1980s, mostly without success, to hire a professional director, secure grants, and establish a more credible facility, at one point even proposing an eighteen-story cultural center to be built on the site, an idea few people in town took seriously, but one symptomatic of the inflated ambitions that living in Las Vegas can produce. In 1995 the city reallocated use of park lands, and the museum was forced to move. The board began looking for another permanent home.

During the early 1990s the Las Vegas–Clark County Library District had begun an ambitious expansion program under the direction of its chief, Charles Hunsberger. Architects such as Robert Graves and Antoine Predock were commissioned, and among the new facilities was one to be built on West Sahara Boulevard. Included was a twelve-thousand-square-foot museum space. Despite attempts by community members involved in other visual arts organizations in town, notably the Nevada Institute for Contemporary Art, to gain access to the new space, the LVAM proposed the management plan that was accepted. After its move in 1997 to the West Sahara Library, the museum saw its visitation grow from around 2,500 per year in Lorenzi Park to more than 60,000 in 2000–2001 at the new venue, mostly the result of sharing a lobby with a large and active library.

The board has managed in recent years to hire two professional directors. Despite its becoming an affiliate of the Smithsonian Institution, a relationship that allows it to rent affordable exhibitions, the LVAM has at best a spotty programming record and has never even begun any serious collecting of the art of the region, much less of the country. One of its few attempts at a local connection was an exhibition in the spring of 2001 of more than 350 works by Dale Chihuly, attempting to piggyback on the fame of his piece in the Bellagio lobby, which had received national press. The show, handsome but expensive to mount, received favorable local press and was well attended but offered little in the way of historical context for the work, and no critical apparatus.

When I visited the museum earlier this year, a volunteer pointed to the doors of the storage area and suggested that I might want to take a look inside, a suggestion that caused me to raise an eyebrow at the obvious breach of security—but in I went. Leaning against the walls was a motley collection of the artworks made by members of the co-op decades ago, as well as posters, prints, and photographs of more recent vintage. The storage area had the feel more of a closet for props at a theater than of the permanent collection of an art museum.

Marianne Lorenz, a professional director the museum lured to Las Vegas from the Yellowstone Art Center, established a solid collegial relationship with Barbara Bloemink during their brief tenures, and the Guggenheim lent staff to help install LVAM shows. The beginning of a fruitful collaboration was in place, but both people moved on to other things. Bloemink became the curatorial director at the Cooper-Hewitt, National Design Museum in New York City. Lorenz, who was beginning to put together an excellent local and regional exhibition program in 2002, was unable to match financial resources to community needs, a systemic problem familiar to anyone who has tried to run a nonprofit arts organization in Las Vegas without the long-term backing of a wealthy patron or two (usually casino owners).

One of the problems the LVAM faces is that, although it receives a generous subsidy for its housing via forgiveness on rent (it pays the library district a dollar a year), the organization's operating budget is not a line item in the city or county budgets. Although there is a city arts commission, it is limited by charter to supporting primarily public art commissions. Furthermore, the county's Cultural

Affairs Division runs its own modest galleries to show contemporary local art, and the combined city-county library system actually manages to maintain its own very small permanent collection. Not only are the two local governmental entities thus in competition to some extent with the museum, but neither offer grants to support it. Overall, public funding of the arts in Las Vegas is dismal on both an absolute and a per capita basis. The art critic Robert Hughes, in a segment of his 1981 Public Broadcasting System series about the history of modern art, *The Shock of the New,* famously stood under the Flamingo's extravagant neon sign and declared that Las Vegas would never have an art museum. How could it, he asked rhetorically and gesturing upwards, compete with this? Even such stalwarts on the local arts scene as Danny Greenspun, who with his wife Robin owns one of the better private art collections in town, think that now only the casinos are up to the job.

Their reasoning is anchored in Nevada's demographics and libertarian tax structure. Las Vegas is a place where roughly nine thousand people move in per month yet three thousand leave. Despite such incredible turnover, the Greater Las Vegas area, most of which lies within the county and not the city itself, almost doubled its population during the 1980s. This demographic fluidity does not inculcate a deep attachment to place, much less a willingness to donate a large percentage of one's income to local cultural amenities. Retirees, for example, will often donate sooner to the nonprofits in their former hometowns, where they grew up and raised families, than here.

The nature of the Las Vegas population is also a challenge for fund-raisers of either private or public funds. As Hal Rothman, an environmental historian at UNLV, points out in his book on the city, *Neon Metropolis,* in 1988 there were more than 313,000 schoolchildren under the age of eighteen in the county, and 500,000 retirees, out of a total population of 1,246,000. Those kinds of disproportions, which continue today, produce a demand for social services without the votes or the demographics to support either serious public financing of local nonprofit art organizations or consistent private gifts.

Nevada's taxes are among the most regressive in the nation: people in lower income brackets pay a disproportionately large share of taxes compared with people who make more money. This imbalance stems from a constitutional clause prohibiting a state income tax, and a property tax that is suppressed down to ankle level. The state's general revenue fund receives almost half of its monies from gaming taxes—although they are the lowest in the country—and another 25 percent or so from a regressive sales tax. The theory and practice is that Las Vegas tourists should and do pay for almost every key infrastructure in the state. Not only is this an abject refusal by Nevadans to take personal responsibility for their own well-being (an oft-noted problem with libertarian politics), but because the tourists now spend more money in Las Vegas on things other than gambling, such as dining and shopping, it subjects the state's treasury to fluctuations in sales tax, which in turn are keyed to consumer confidence, not a very stable ground upon which to forecast revenues.

Rothman has traced how lack of funding has forced the Las Vegas city and Clark County governments to steadily abrogate responsibilities for civic infrastructure—such as roads and sidewalks and education—to the private sector. This is a trend becoming more widespread nationally, as the demographics for schoolchildren and older people in America come to mirror more closely those of Las Vegas. The arts in Las Vegas remain underfunded at all levels—support of arts education in the schools, commissions for public art, subsidies of ticket prices to performances, and construction and maintenance of facilities, including the LVAM.

The forgiveness of rent by the library district for the museum is therefore a rare, welcome, and well-intentioned gesture, but it has also placed the museum in a double bind. According to Lorenz, as well as the current director, Karen Barrett, its twelve-thousand-square-foot space is completely inadequate. The library building is a rich lexicon of contemporary architectural forms: vaulted geometries, asymmetrical piercings, and visual allusions to local geography are a few of its many pleasures. But because museum professionals didn't design the exhibition facility, the gallery is far too tall for the width of its exhibition sightlines. Its floor footage is sufficient for a gallery that receives and mounts small exhibitions but hopelessly cramped for a genuine museum, which is to say for an institution that actually collects, stores, and preserves a permanent collection. It also lacks spaces for arts-education classes and retail, depriving it of an opportunity to earn revenues. Furthermore, it is enslaved in a house that it does not own. Museums in America do best when they build and own their own facilities, which makes them more attractive to donors.

As a result, the museum has never had the opportunity to try and build a citywide network of support around construction of a building, an edifice, the easiest fund-raising vehicle that exists. It has thus remained unable to maintain a consistently professional staff, much less conduct any long-range strategic planning to change its situation. The mentality of being a closely held collective formed for mutual profit still pervades its behavior. Joe Palermo, who has served on both the board and staff of the museum, stepped in as acting director shortly after Lorenz left. A few months later he resigned his position, handed off the reins to another board member (while maintaining an advisory status to the board), and went into business running a private gallery. The next exhibition of the museum was a show by Marlene Tseng Yu. A concurrent exhibit of her work also appeared at Palermo's newly incorporated Southern Nevada Museum of Fine Art, which is billed in its brochure as a "privately funded non-profit organization" but is in reality a limited-liability, private, for-profit corporation. Ads for both exhibitions appeared in *Art in America* and *Artforum*. The less-than-professional photographs of Tseng Yu standing in front of her work lead one to wonder whether, given the lack of a budget at the LVAM, the artist paid for the ads herself.

Although Palermo insists that his storefront business, funded by a local businessman, Jerry Polis, another LVAM board member, is not a selling gallery, and no request is made of visitors for donations, the circumstances might be construed to constitute a conflict of interest. Palermo neatly creates what is legally defined as a for-profit venue for work being promoted by the LVAM — work that he helped select — then shows work by the same artist at the same time in a misleadingly designated business and reaps whatever benefits he chooses, whether they be monetary or social. The language in his mission statement, printed in the gallery's brochure, is identical to the words used by the LVAM's curator, James Mann: to "stress Art after Postmodernism."

What Palermo is doing, however ambiguous its intention, is similar to what Wynn has arranged for the galleries in his resorts. Palermo's calling his gallery a museum is ostensibly no less confusing than the Guggenheim-Hermitage's doing the same thing. The behavior of all four venues brings up some interesting questions about not only the value of art, but the nature of what is private and public. If Wynn, whose corporation owned the pedestrian walkways in front of the Bellagio, had decided to display a painting by van Gogh in a thick glass box out on the sidewalk, would that have been public art or private? The public would have been viewing it for free, but the sidewalk was patrolled by his private security guards, who seek to move along those whose presence he deemed inappropriate—as he tried to do in 1999 to people handing out advertisements for escort services. Whose view is it, anyway? Wynn lost his battle, which the courts defined as an issue of free speech.

〜 Elaine and Steve Wynn were, and remain, two of the more important individual patrons of the arts in Las Vegas, helping to fund ballet and symphony performances, visual art exhibitions, and so on. Like most Americans, however, they prefer to make their donations as individuals at a local level and not channel their philanthropy through anonymous government grants filtered by peer panel review. This kind of giving—a particularly American brand of philanthropy—has allowed them to purchase with honor an exalted place in society, just as it did for earlier captains of other industries, such as John D. Rockefeller, Henry Clay Frick, Andrew Mellon, and J. Paul Getty, and as it does for Bill Gates today.

The American economy has three sectors: the private, for-profit business world, the government, and the private, not-for-profit or nonprofit "civic society." The roots of the nonprofit sector arise from the idea that a society can and should establish formal mechanisms and organizations to redistribute wealth voluntarily for humanitarian purposes, thus balancing the sometimes predatory behavior of business, and filling the holes left in the safety net by politicians. Societies as early as the ancient Egyptians, Greeks, and Romans established endowments to promote learning and education, the library at Alexandria being but one example. During medieval times, European society relied mostly on religious orders to serve this purpose, echoes of which are still with us in government funding for "faith-based initiatives," which are grants to nonprofit churches. Charity, a word meaning Christian love, first came to imply giving to support the poor; the Augustinian and Benedictine orders established rules not only for almshouses but also for the support of monasteries and hospitals. By 1601 England's Queen Elizabeth I was promulgating an even more secular Statute of Charitable Uses, which encouraged gifts for everything from the support of scholars in universities to the building of bridges.

The strong separation of church and government in the American Constitution (which makes the public funding of faith-based programs run by churches a controversial idea) led to the development of a secular network of charities. The first organized fundraiser in America, although it was still labeled begging at the time, was held by Harvard University in 1643, but widespread philanthropy didn't really blossom until the Civil War created a need for private funds to augment government spending on both wounded soldiers and war-related public health problems. The consequent outpouring of individual giving in turn helped spur the founding of the American Red Cross in 1881, the first large-scale and national nonprofit public charity in the country.

At the same time, a postwar stratum of millionaires flourished in American society. By 1880 there were approximately one hundred such wealthy individuals; in 1916 there were more than forty thousand. Andrew Carnegie published an essay in 1889 urging the rich to spread their wealth through public trusts, versus leaving the money to their families, and in 1891 John D. Rockefeller Sr. hired a staff to administer his philanthropy. In 1913 Rockefeller's fortune surpassed $900 million, at which point he established a foundation. This was, not coincidentally, the year that the federal income tax as we know it was established. During Rockefeller's lifetime, he donated an estimated $500 million to charitable and educational organizations.

Carnegie, Frick, Rockefeller, Mellon, and Henry Ford were heads of great corporations, and it was only logical that they should turn to the for-profit business structure as a model for their foundations: a board of directors would oversee the management and distribution of the funds. The federal income tax climbed steeply to support the entrance of America into World War I in 1917, and the industrialists brokered a deal with the government allowing them to deduct up to 15 percent of their taxable income for charitable gifts. The provision for deductions of income tax, a parallel provision in the Estate Tax Act of 1921, and the subsequent Gift Tax Act of 1932 allowed the millionaires to avoid or offset capital gains taxes on appreciating stocks, as well as lower their estate taxes, thus preserving the corpus of family wealth.

Likewise, nonprofit organizations organized themselves with boards of directors, providing some measure of organizational symmetry between grantmaker and applicant. Those nonprofits that registered with the Internal Revenue Service and could prove their educational and charitable benefit to society could gain tax-exempt status, which allowed them to operate without paying most taxes. Even more important, these nonprofits provided places for small businesses and even individuals of modest means to donate funds, goods, and services for a tax deduction. The increasing organization of arts venues, such as New York's Metropolitan Museum of Art and Boston's Museum of Fine Art, to nonprofit status shifted their management styles from impresario to business administrator.

During the 1960s the number of all nonprofit organizations began to boom, but in particular, numerous arts groups sprang into being because of public financing by agencies such as the National Endowment for the Arts and its smaller siblings, the state arts agencies. Then, as government funding for social needs begin to be curtailed during the Reagan and Bush years, the nonprofits were seen increasingly as a cost-effective mechanism for meeting those needs. In 1996, for example, 1.27 million of the more than 1.5 million nonprofits were tax-exempt, and their revenues were $621.4 billion, or 7 percent of the nation's business revenues. Total direct charitable giving in America in 2002 totaled $240 billion, and more than 80 percent of all charitable giving to nonprofits came from individuals. Americans are the most charitable people on a per capita basis in the world, but they prefer the control of that giving to remain in their own hands, not those of the government.

On top of direct support, Americans also support nonprofits by forgiving the amount of taxes that would otherwise be collected from both the donors and the organizations. Eighty-six percent of all museums and botanical and zoological gardens are nonprofits. When Americans complain that government doesn't support, say, the arts at the level of some European countries, they are forgetting to add federal tax forgiveness to the level of direct grants, which brings the United States to a level of support on par with that of the most generous countries in Europe. (Many European governments, which do not provide tax relief for contributions to nonprofits, increasingly express an interest in the American system.)

The combination of low state corporate taxes on the hotel and gaming industries in Nevada and the federal incentives for individual giving help explain why Steve and Elaine Wynn vociferously opposed the legislature's raising the state room tax even a fraction of 1 percent in the late 1980s to fund the state's cultural agencies—a tax that would have created more cultural attractions, thus more reasons for tourists to visit the state, thus more revenue for the hotels. The tax measure failed to pass. Several years later Wynn and his wife spent a half billion dollars buying art and the legislature gave them a tax break for doing so. By blurring the lines between profit and nonprofit behavior, and seeking to have the tax laws accommodate them, the Wynns maximize profit, retain control of their personal culture, and foster a libertarian capitalism based on individual rights.

Manipulating art and taxes is not an unusual strategy for wealthy art patrons. Andrew Mellon, a powerful banker, opponent of income taxes, and early proponent of the trickle-down theory of prosperity, bought twenty-one paintings from the Hermitage in the early 1930s and deducted their nearly $7-million purchase price from his income taxes—while serving as the secretary of the treasury during the Great Depression. The subsequent government investigations were called off only when he finally donated the works in 1937—works which for years he had denied even buying—to what would become the National Gallery of Art. The California industrialist Norton Simon bought more than twelve *thousand* works of art in his lifetime, loaned them to museums out of state to avoid sales tax, kept them available for resale, and eventually completed a hostile takeover of the Pasadena Art Museum in the early 1970s. He renamed it the Norton Simon Museum, installed his works, and remained firmly in control of it even after contracting a progressively debilitating neurological disorder. The museum had a European painting collection the depth and quality of which were arguably higher than the Getty's. Getty himself was donating art during the mid-1970s equal in value to half his gross annual income. In 1975, the year after he opened his Villa museum, he gave $14.7 million in art against an income of $29.4 million, upon which he paid income tax of only $4.2 million, or about 14 percent. As Robert Lenzner put it in his book about Getty, "Not bad for the richest man in the world."

During the last six months of 2003 Steve Wynn both bought and sold the two most expensive artworks offered at auction worldwide that year. Like his wealthy predecessors, he is a major force driving the international art market, but more than Mellon or Frick, Simon or Getty, he is also a potentially significant agent in the shaping of the larger American culture. Because he has the public laboratory of Las Vegas in which to experiment with the roles of profit and nonprofit business in the presentation of culture, his actions are witnessed by millions—including Thomas Krens, Sheldon Adelson, and others who are encouraged consequently to try their own experiments.

As artists increasingly adopt mass culture as the source material for their fine art, thus helping make permeable the barriers separating high and low cultures in America, so the values we attribute to profit and nonprofit businesses begin to merge. Wynn, despite being accused of manipulating the state legislature for his favorable tax treatment, is also lauded for the innovation of bringing fine art onto the Strip. Krens, while accused of pandering to commercial interests with his motorcycle and Armani exhibitions, is admired for his ability to turn the word *Guggenheim* into a brand name for a museum. Overall, however, we tend to think that Krens is taking a step down and Wynn a step up in the hierarchy of social legitimacy. The museum is considered to be stepping down from high art and the casino climbing up, despite the fact that the difference between the two is not as large as we might think.

⌇ One reason the Getty was so overwhelmed with visitors was that its price tag was widely touted to be a billion dollars. The Bellagio was publicized to cost $1.6 billion. The monuments of wealth are a spectacle because they are the "largest," the "most beautiful," and the "most expensive." We assume by fiat of superlative that they will outlast the individuals who built them, a foundational principle of religion since at least the erection of earthen funerary mastabas in Mesopotamia 5,500 years ago and their more sophisticated stone counterparts, the pyramids of Egypt, starting a thousand years later—both the largest structures built by their societies. No one expects the pyramid at the Luxor hotel-casino to last more than a few decades, nor do tourists expect that the hand-painted ceilings of the Venetian will last as long as the Sistine Chapel's. But they do expect that the single most valuable items in the Venetian, the Bellagio, and Wynn Las Vegas—the paintings that cost millions of dollars—will be cared for in perpetuity as they pass from one pair of hands to another. The paintings are talismans of immortality.

Most tourists, when paying $15 to enter the galleries, are not there to contemplate the meanings of the paintings as intended by their artists, but the meaning as intended by their owners. It's the allure of wealth as spectacle that is at least the initial attraction, the fact of standing in the presence of objects that we revere as being closer to immortality than anything we ourselves own. The gallery owners, even as they display paintings such as Steen's *In Luxury Beware*, which is an admonishment against greed, lust, and gluttony, are reveling in the fact that artworks have a long history as commodities. And so, as audiences, are we.

The branding of art collections proceeds by naming the arena in which the spectacle is presented after the name of the impresario who collected the artworks—the Frick, the Guggenheim, the Getty, the Wynn. So it is no longer the "Museum of Modern Art" or "Boston Museum of Fine Art," designations that declare the egos of the individual patrons and donors subordinate to a movement in art history or a civic entity, which is to say to an idea, or even an ideal. Now, instead, we have a celebration of the fact that an individual, by amassing these works, can create a spectacle and thus transcend his or her own limitations as an individual by influencing the larger society and its culture—and thereby gain a small advantage over mortality.

Spectacle is about participating in an event or sight that is larger than ourselves and, by complicit association with the wealthy individual, emphasizing a relationship to immortality. We witness something we take to be of greater import than ourselves, or than the moment, and believe we have touched something more fundamental to the universe. And we do so with minimal effort on our part, paying only the price of admission.

How the casinos use art to sell themselves can surprise even the most jaded visitor, as with Jenny Holzer's aphorism "Protect me from what I want" on the Caesars marquee. The 1986 *Truisms* project was publicly funded and administered by a nonprofit organization (the now-defunct Nevada Institute for Contemporary Art) but run on the board as part of the spectacle of the Strip even as the words sought to subvert the rationale of the setting. Caesars later went on to work with the state arts council to show other artworks on its marquee, ranging from the miniature erotic needlepoint tapestries of D. R. Wagner to announcing a conceptual wedding of the Statue of Liberty with the statue of Columbus in Barcelona by the Spanish artist Antonio Miralda. What was intriguing about these projects was that they were by artists whose names were not recognizable to the vast majority of the public, and the artworks played off of and lambasted greed, lust, and colonialism. Caesars had nothing direct to gain monetarily from putting the works on the marquee and in fact went to considerable staff time and trouble to do so. What was it selling, if anything?

Apart from the explanation offered me by the management— that they simply got a kick out of showing their counterparts on the Strip that Caesars was a more sophisticated establishment—I found these marquee postings a subtle but clear allusion to a European sensibility about culture via the art market of New York. It was a way of saying to well-traveled high rollers that Caesars was part of a world culture that had more reach and staying power than the aging pop stars on the other hotel-casinos' marquees. It said that Caesars was a cut above it all, that it was secure enough in its market niche to posit the ironies.

Another example in town is the art collection of the Rio Hotel and Casino, a resort off the Strip built and once owned by Anthony Marnell, the chairman of Marnell Carrao, the local construction firm that builds most of the major resorts in town, including the

Mirage and Wynn Las Vegas. Although most of the Rio's public areas are themed after the city for which it is named, it contains one of the largest corporate art collections in the state. The hotel's ultra-luxe "Palazzo" suites are reserved for "whales," the top hundred or so gamblers in the world, who will play up to a hundred thousand dollars a hand and drop a million in an evening. Each of the suites has an extensive backstory underlying its decoration, which is then illustrated with art to match: excellent eighteenth-century European landscape paintings, rare jade pieces, small works by Renoir, Picasso, Hockney—whatever it takes to create not the illusion of luxury, but the actuality.

But it was in the public spaces in and around the hotel's convention center and theater that the Rio took an unexpected leap. In the spacious corridor leading from the meeting rooms to the casino, Marnell Carrao's executive vice president for design, Lee Cagley, installed works by Richard Serra, Jasper Johns, Cy Twombly, Ellsworth Kelly, April Gornik, Gerhard Richter, Jennifer Bartlett, and other art-world luminaries alongside works by Las Vegas artists Jose Bellver, Mary Warner, Robert Beckmann, Joanne Vuillemot, and Jim Pink. Cagley included photography as well, ranging once again from works by locals such as the UNLV instructor Pasha Rafat to the internationally known artists Richard Misrach and Uta Barth.

Here, too, the casino stood to make no direct profit from putting these works in view of the public. But for years the Rio was known as a casino for locals, and the artworks were part of the marketing strategy. By placing works by the best artists in town next to pieces by their more widely known peers, Cagley had begun to create a curatorial context for local contemporary art that is so far unmatched anywhere else in Las Vegas. In essence, the Rio was promoting local pride, albeit in a way not likely to be obvious to all the patrons.

It is probably too much to expect the current owners of the Rio, Harrah's Entertainment, which seems to have little interest in the collection, to donate the local artists's works in it to the Las Vegas Art Museum. But if the board of the museum could shake off its parochial roots and locate a patron willing and able to buy that part of the collection then turn around and give it to museum for a substantial tax deduction, the city and its residents would have been partially repaid for the low gaming taxes paid by the casino.

〜〜 It's not any one individual who has much chance of longevity, much less immortality, but the culture as a whole, which we usually judge over historical time to be represented in large measure by its artworks. If Las Vegas hopes to maintain a place in history, moving these talismans out of private and into public hands is a prerequisite, given that the architecture of the Strip rests on planned obsolescence.

OF LIONS AND TIGERS

As he had done 5,749 times before, the perpetually young-at-heart and tanned Roy Horn walked out onto the stage of the Mirage showroom halfway through the Siegfried & Roy show. It was a Friday evening, the entertainer's fifty-ninth birthday, and at the point in the show when it was time to bring out Montecore, the act's signature animal. The six-hundred-pound white tiger, a cat so large that when it stands on its hind legs it can put its front paws over the top of a nine-foot fence, trailed behind Horn on a short leash. In a few minutes Horn and his partner, Siegfried Fischbacher, were due to make the huge animal disappear before the audience in a fountain of fireworks. Every one of the showroom's fifteen hundred seats was taken, as they had been six nights a week for forty-five weeks a year since February of 1990. Horn told the audience that this was Montecore's debut, a fabrication he used every night to make the audience feel especially privileged. Then he told the big cat to lie down. The tiger refused.

Eyewitness accounts differ, as they will, saying either that Horn pulled at the leash as a command for the cat to lie down or that the entertainer stumbled—but everyone agrees that Montecore grabbed him by the forearm without any warning. Horn began thumping the cat on the head with a live microphone, saying "No, no." He ended up on the ground with the amplified thumps from the microphone still echoing in the theater while the tiger hauled him offstage by the neck. The most commonly used description of the event said that Horn looked like a "rag doll" in the tiger's jaws. Patrons could hear him screaming behind the curtains.

The handlers backstage emptied a fire extinguisher on the cat, who relinquished Horn with reluctance, and a stagehand quickly stanched the massive flow of blood from the left side of the magician's neck. The bite had just missed his carotid artery. Horn was taken to a trauma center and stabilized, then moved to Los Angeles for treatment. It will be years—if ever—before he recovers from the muscular and neurological damage caused by the bite, as well as a stroke and swelling of the brain suffered soon after the incident. Montecore was put into quarantine for ten days, as required by law, and observed for evidence of disease or odd behavior. Nothing was noted, and he was released back into the Secret Garden, the facility behind the Mirage where the pair's sixty-three exotic cats live. The 267 employees who worked on the Siegfried & Roy show were let go one week after the accident, management declaring that the production was over.

According to the local journalist Ed Koch, writing in the *Las Vegas Sun* shortly after the attack, maulings by tigers had occurred before in Las Vegas. Charlie Stagnaro, a sixty-five-year-old trainer at the Keepers of the Wild sanctuary, was feeding a Bengal tiger when it attacked, and Eric Bloom was killed in 2001 at a private (and illegal) facility on Mount Charleston, west of the city, when another Bengal took him by the neck. Koch discovered that in that same year a handler in Florida was killed by a Siberian tiger, again with a bite to the neck, a typical killing method for the animals. Local television noted that a man working at Siegfried and Roy's big-cat compound at their house was left paralyzed in 1985 when one of the tigers grabbed him the same way. But it took the mauling of Roy Horn to end an era in Las Vegas entertainment.

Siegfried Fischbacher was born in Rosenheim, Bavaria, in 1939, and Horn in Nordenham, near Bremen, in 1944. In 1953 the former gave his first public performance of magic, failing miserably at an attempt to make a goat disappear in front of a farmers' group. Not long afterward, Horn was frequenting the Bremen zoo and making friends with a two-year-old cheetah named Chico. In 1959 the two met aboard a cruise ship, where Fischbacher was the ship's entertainer and Horn a steward. When Horn saw that Fischbacher was making rabbits and doves disappear during his act, he realized that perhaps he could do the same for a cheetah. Fischbacher agreed, Chico came aboard, and Siegfried and Roy were born as both a romantic couple and as a stage act.

In 1967 the trio arrived in Las Vegas with a second cheetah and a flamingo in tow and debuted with a twelve-minute act at the Tropicana as part of the Trop's fabled "Folies Bergere" show. They returned to Las Vegas in 1970 to perform a fifteen-minute act in the Stardust's "Lido" production and slowly worked their way into larger venues with longer performances until in 1978 they received star billing to provide a thirty-minute finale. They were now the highest-paid specialty act on the Strip, and in 1982 they negotiated a full-length show at the Frontier that was the first ongoing magic show on the Strip. That same year they acquired three white tiger cubs, two from the Cincinnati Zoo, and begin to breed them.

According to the Humane Society of the United States, the first white tiger was a female brought into the country in 1960 by the National Zoo. She was subsequently bred and her offspring distributed around the country. White tigers—which actually have white fur with faint chocolate stripes—are chance mutations resulting from recessive genes, and none has ever been observed in the wild. Presumably this is because their coloration provides them with little of the camouflage they rely on both to elude detection when young and to hunt their prey when mature. Being white is hardly a favorable mutation for tiger survival.

The Humane Society estimates that as many as fifteen thousand big cats of various species are kept by private citizens in the United States as pets. Between five thousand and seven thousand tigers are here in captivity, with less than 10 percent of them in professionally maintained zoos and sanctuaries. The rest live in circuses, big-cat rescue operations, and backyards (or, in one case, much to the dismay of the police in late 2003, the bedroom of a New York City apartment). Most people purchase their big cats online, with a regular tiger cub costing as little as $500 and a white Siberian going for as much as $100,000. Organizations such as People for the Ethical Treatment of Animals (PETA) worry that within a few years, as the cats mature, two things will happen. Cats will escape and become a danger to the public, making them a target for law enforcement (as was the case in New York), and cats will increasingly be sold to private hunting preserves, making them a target for trophy hunters. In the majority of both cases, the cats will lose their lives.

Unfortunately, tigers raised in captivity cannot be released into the wild, as they lack the requisite survival skills. Furthermore, the only white tigers in the world are bred in captivity and, contrary to popular belief, are not a separate species or an especially endangered one (they are actually Bengal tigers, the most numerous of all the subspecies). Because the whites are inbred, they suffer from congenital defects such as club feet, severe hip dysplasia, and cataracts. Even if they could be released, they would lower the robustness of the already fragile gene pool shared by the estimated five thousand tigers living in the wild, some subspecies of which (such as the Siberian and Sumatran) are genuinely endangered.

Despite these realities the public is entranced by the white tigers, and when Steve Wynn signed Fischbacher and Horn to a $57.5 million contract to open the Mirage, he was purchasing the best act on the Strip that money could buy. He wanted to offer his patrons entertainment that did not feature nudity or overt sex, thus increasing the appeal of the resort to women. Siegfried and Roy, building upon the legacy of Liberace with their pretty-boy looks and glittering costumes, substituted coded flamboyance for sex, which fit perfectly with Wynn's aesthetic rationale behind building the first luxury resort on the Strip without neon.

The duo opened in 1990 in a glitzy spectacular, their costumes and sets designed by John Napier, an associate designer of the Royal Shakespeare Company who had also done the costumes and sets for *Cats* and *Les Misérables* on Broadway. The show was an instant sold-out hit and redefined what was possible for family entertainment in Las Vegas. Six years later the two moved the animals from their private residence, the "Jungle Palace," to the Secret Garden and Dolphin Habitat, a new habitat and attraction at the Mirage.

When Roy Horn walked out onstage with Montecore, each of the fifteen hundred patrons watching him had paid an average of $100 per ticket, and the ticket gross for the evening would be about $157,000. During its run, the show earned almost $45 million in annual sales. Overall, the Mirage was generating about $150 million in annual cash flow, of which only $5 million came from the show after expenses—but it wasn't the direct earnings that mattered as much as the draw of the spectacle, a production in which elephants disappeared in midair above the stage. An estimated 10.5 million patrons had seen the show, most of whom ate at restaurants in the Mirage and dropped some money on the tables.

Although many of the duo's sixty-three exotic cats remained on view in the Secret Garden attraction out back and the gift shop remained open, fourth-quarter gaming revenues and food and beverage sales the year of the attack did, indeed, drop. Not disastrously, but noticeably.

A few days after the attack I visited the Mirage with my partner, Karen Smith, with whom I live in the equestrian district of Burbank. Karen rides and jumps horses. She has no aversion to humans and animals working together in close proximity but is deeply conflicted about even domestic animals being confined too closely, much less wild ones being kept in captivity. The protesters outside the Mirage did nothing to lighten her apprehensions.

~~ "Retire the Tigers" reads one sign. "The Strip Is No Place for Tigers" proclaims another. The fifteen or so members of PETA are quiet, and the reaction of most people entering the long passageway from the sidewalk to the casino is one of either determined avoidance or mild curiosity. After all, almost everyone else is using this entrance precisely in order to see one of the white tigers on display in a large glassed-in enclosure to our left. On the other side is the gift shop, stuffed to overflowing with plush jungle cats in an assortment of sizes from miniature to considerably larger than your average ten-year-old child.

A single white male lounges on a ledge in the habitat, a teaser for the Secret Garden, and hundreds of people press against the glass, murmuring in awe. Above our heads video monitors run a tape of Siegfried and Roy playing with tiger cubs at home. It's either the same tape, or one very similar to it, that I watched here two years ago, and I can't help wondering if a new one will be substituted soon. The Mirage has announced that although the show will be closed, the Secret Garden and the tigers will remain as attractions.

It takes a few minutes of determined hiking through most of the casino to reach the elevated breezeway on the opposite side of the resort, a shaded path that leads to the entrance of the habitats for the cats and the dolphins. To the left is what passes for a hotel pool these days in Las Vegas. It's actually more of an artificial beach than a swimming pool, its sides carefully oriented for the display of sunbathers to one another. The adult water park is nonetheless a traditional architectural expression of the tropical island paradise theme to be found in Las Vegas, with 2.5 million gallons of reconstituted seawater flowing through two enormous lagoons, the larger of which is twenty-two feet deep. Fifty other people stand in line with us for a few minutes until it's our turn to follow a guide through the ficus and palms to the edge of the first enclosure.

Our guide informs us that seven of the ten Atlantic bottlenose dolphins at the Mirage were born on-site and stresses that the facility does not stage shows, but that there are frequent "interactions" between the animals and the staff as the latter conduct research and educational activities. I wonder about the nature of the research being conducted. More than five hundred dolphins are listed online in the captive dolphin database, most of them at commercial entertainment facilities that deploy a similar rhetoric in order to assuage the public's guilt about holding such intelligent mammals—meaning creatures uncomfortably like ourselves—in captivity.

Karen and I break from the crowd and circulate around the pools, the dolphins leaping and twisting in the air, playing with toys, and being admirably charismatic—exactly as they were when I last visited. Approximately sixty thousand schoolchildren visit here annually, and the Mirage sponsors an internship program with the UNLV Department of Environmental Studies. Staff and interns at the facility have investigated matters ranging from dolphin behavior, breeding, and artificial insemination to dolphin-assisted therapy for autistic children. The founding director of the facility, marine biologist Julie Wignall, was not given much direction when contacted by Wynn, other than to bring dolphins to the desert, and she kept the dual goals of research and entertainment well in mind.

Still, it's obvious that the marine animals are trained to play with balls, walk on their tails, and to vocalize and wave their flippers when cued to do so, which are the stock-in-trade tricks of commercial venues such as Sea World. What distresses Karen as we rejoin our group is not that the animals are being mistreated, but that they are removed from their natural environment. The unexpected juxtaposition of desert and dolphins implies the wealth and power necessary to produce such a sight, which creates the spectacle that Wynn wanted: a display of how he has the resources to overcome the conventions of geography, just as he does with tax laws.

While the guide is still talking to the group about how the local desert water is treated to make it habitable for the dolphins, we once again slip away, this time to enter the Secret Garden. While the dolphin environment is open and relatively utilitarian—the pipes and pumps of the recirculation plant deliberately left visible as a mechanical analog for the seriousness of the endeavor—the Secret Garden is much more of a theme park. A soundtrack with drums and flutes plays softly in the background, sounding a bit more like South America than either Africa or a South Seas island, but it's stereotypically exotic and equatorial.

We stop first at the elephant enclosure where a fifty-five-year-old Asian pachyderm named Gildah is kept. A trainer is in the large pen, urging her toward a shallow pool while offering small treats and pats on the flank and trunk. Elephants are intensely social animals, and PETA has petitioned the Mirage to send Gildah to a sanctuary where she can be with other elephants in a large park, but to no avail.

We continue resolutely past white lions and tigers, a leopard, and a black panther. The overall environment is pleasant and seemingly spacious for a series of cages located a block from the Strip, but the cats display what zoologists label "stereotypical pacing," a sign that they are stressed by not having available a wide-ranging habitat. Two teenage girls press up against the wire separating the crowd from the black panther, who rests on a ledge at the back of the pen. They yell at the cat to wake up and do something. It's more than likely they're unaware that three years ago the tigers here had chewed through the wire and were restrained by keepers only minutes before the facility opened to the public for the day.

As we come up to the rear apex of the path and start back, Karen grabs my arm and points: a tiny brown field mouse runs from under one of the benches and pauses to sniff the air. Karen gently shoos it back into the shrubs. No one else seems to have noticed the only genuine wildlife here, and she's worried that someone might step on it.

As we leave, I stop to examine the *Twenty-first Century Ark of Noah* mural by Franciscan nuns in Romania. A plaque states that one of Siegfried's sisters is a member of the group, which blesses the work that the entertainers are doing on behalf of conservation. I can't help but note that bottlenose dolphins are no more an endangered species than are the white tigers, and that the preservation of species and a diverse and viable gene pool for them in zoos is a fairly recent idea with decidedly mixed results. Your average American zoo owns around fifty-three species, most of them large vertebrates, a group that overall makes up only 56,000 of the total 30 million species estimated to be alive (most of them very small and decidedly not visually spectacular or charismatic at all—think bugs). The United Nations lists at least 5,400 species as threatened. As the zoo architect and historian David Hancocks points out in his book *A Different Nature*, if all the professional zoos in the world put half their budgets toward saving those threatened, they might be able to maintain breeding populations for 800 of them. Yet the majority of Americans believe that the most important role of zoos is to save animals from extinction, a fact of which anyone who administers the budget for a zoological attraction is quite aware.

〜 The history of zoos is a manifestation of how we view our relationship to nature, and it displays the ambivalence we have in accepting that we, too, are animals. Putting up a fence between a human and a tiger is a sensible precaution, but it also reinforces a sense of hierarchy—that we are more valuable in the scheme of things because we have freedom of movement and the tiger does not. Exercising power over an imprisoned animal makes us the conqueror and the colonizer of the planet, a less-than-useful viewpoint when trying to maintain the viability of species, including our own.

The word *zoo* was derived from the Greek *zoion*, which means "living being," but there is a clear distinction between a menagerie, which is a collection of animals kept for personal purposes, and a zoo, which we now more commonly associate with an organized public collection maintained for educational and research purposes. There are more than fifteen hundred zoos worldwide and countless menageries; the Secret Garden falls somewhere between the two.

The first animals held in group captivity were, presumably, those kept in pens for purposes of domesticating them, but the earliest evidence of animals in collections are records of aviaries in Mesopotamia around 4500 BC. Egyptian pictographs and hieroglyphs dating from 2500 BC show such species as cheetahs and baboons in the personal menageries of kings, and there is contemporaneous evidence from India that elephants were kept captive. A thousand years later Queen Hatshepsut sent a collecting expedition to the Red Sea region that brought back exotic birds, monkeys, and leopards for her personal amusement. The Chinese emperor Wen Wang founded a 1,500-acre zoo in 1000 BC that he named the Garden of Intelligence, the earliest instance known of a zoo organized for public entertainment and enlightenment.

The ancient city-states of Greece maintained educational zoos, and during the fourth century BC Aristotle researched taxonomy using a menagerie established during Alexander the Great's conquests. Some decades later Ptolemy II in Egypt paraded exotic animals in religious processions. It was under the Romans, however, that the collection of both art and animals became a spectacle. During four centuries of conquest they raided not only the ancient civilizations of the Mediterranean but the forest and jungles as well. The private collections of art became so popular that the owners opened their houses to the public on a regular basis, and during the first century AD the emperors of Rome had the most significant pieces nationalized.

When we think of "spectacle," one of the first examples that comes to mind is the ancient Roman use of wild animals in arenas. As in the Roman art world, the popularity of private menageries led to public events, and the government began to sponsor staged fights between animals, between animals and enemies of the state, and between professional gladiators and animals as early as 186 BC. In AD 80 alone, Titus had nine thousand animals killed in amphitheaters, and when the Colosseum was inaugurated, he watched as five thousand died in forced hunts and fights in front of fifty thousand spectators. Bears, elephants, lions, tigers, water buffalo, rhinoceroses, leopards, apes of all kinds, ostriches, bison, seals, crocodiles, even giraffes fell in the arenas to spears, arrows, clubs, and other weapons.

The slaughters were financed by the rulers, the high officers of the Legion, and other wealthy men as proof of wealth and power or as attempts to gain such. The network of suppliers wiped out the elephants in North Africa and lions from Mesopotamia. Simultaneously, rich Romans maintained menageries at their villas for leisurely study, and one built a huge aviary that also served as a dining room. One shouldn't think that the Rainbow Café in the MGM has invented anything new, with people eating lunch below flocks of mechanized birds.

Although Europe did not have public zoos during the medieval ages, Charlemagne in the 800s continued the tradition of the wealthy and powerful trading animals from their menageries to curry political favor and establish their *bona fides* as persons of means and culture. During the thirteenth century the Holy Roman Emperor Frederick II, a serious scholar of birds and animals, collected everything from hyenas to polar bears and sent some animals to his brother-in-law King Henry III, who established his own menagerie in the Tower of London, a prison for wildlife as well as criminals. Staged fights between the animals, blinded beforehand, were conducted at the Tower Zoo as late as the Tudor era.

The collecting of animals has ranged across the world and its cultures throughout history, and even Montezuma maintained a large menagerie in the 1500s. That same century, Renaissance explorers and scholars began to capitalize upon the opening of the New World, and later the islands of the Pacific Ocean, to expand their collections. At first the specimens brought back were merely curiosities to be added to royal collections, but as the number of new species discovered climbed exponentially, scholars insisted on imposing some taxonomic order, which led to both the invention of the natural history museum and the transformation of menageries into zoos available to the public. In 1664 Louis XIV of France established a zoological garden at Versailles that was both open to the public and served as a research facility for scientist. The collection became the basis for the Jardin des Plantes in Paris, which in turn opened a Ménagerie in 1793 that later became the Paris Zoo.

The influence of the Jardin was felt keenly by the competitive British, who established their own Zoological Society of London in 1825; the group soon subsumed the Tower menagerie. Although the Zoological Society was at first interested in determining whether the exotic species could be domesticated for human purposes, by the early nineteenth century it was obvious that the laws passed two hundred years earlier encouraging the extermination of wild-life that might compete against farm animals had meant the almost complete disappearance of any wild beasties larger than a fox from the British Isles. Only the royal hunting preserves still boasted wild habitat with deer, otter, pheasant, and a handful of other species. Zoos and natural history became obsessions with the British, part of the Romantic movement that would carry with it to America the idea that untamed Nature in capital letters was pure and sublime, an antidote to the Industrial Revolution and the decadence of urban society. Hancocks points out that it is no coincidence that the naturalist John Muir, the photographer Eadweard Muybridge, and the painter Thomas Moran were prominent in the establishment of Yosemite Valley as a national park in 1890. All three were expatriate Brits.

Zoos in America began with the establishment of one in Philadelphia in 1874 and the Cincinnati Zoo the next year. The Bronx Zoo, the largest in the country, with approximately six thousand animals, opened in 1889 and was the first to adopt what would become the tripartite mission of modern zoos. Not only was it a place for education and recreation—a place for intimating, if not actually re-creating, an Edenic version of the world—but it was also charged with conservation. Americans, like the British, had a bad habit of hunting species to extinction, such as the passenger pigeon and very nearly the bison. Zoos were seen as places where the public could learn an early version of "wise use" practice.

Throughout most of the nineteenth century zoos competed with one another for not only the largest and most diverse collections of specimens (and that's what the animals were seen as: examples of collecting prowess) but also the most elaborate and exotic architecture. Elephants in Berlin were housed in a *faux* Burmese temple built in 1873, a result of that century's fascination with all things Oriental. Animals elsewhere were housed in replicas of Tudor cottages, Greek temples, Swiss chalets, Renaissance pavilions. These handsome structures weren't really any improvement in quarters for the animals; they were designed for human pleasure based on the *frisson* of seeming to touch a distant and alien culture at the same time as viewing an exotic animal.

It wasn't until after the turn of the century that a zoo built a naturalistic landscape and, furthermore, mixed species in an attempt to provide some semblance of a natural habitat. Carl Hagenbeck opened a private zoo in a Hamburg suburb. He hired a Swiss sculptor, Urs Eggenschwyler, and together they invented the artificial mountain, an advance made possible by the use of concrete, still a relatively new building material. Eggenschwyler designed rocky enclosures based on actual terrain, with a series of moats so the public could enjoy seeing the animals without the intrusion of bars. Both the animals and the visitors were happier with the arrangement.

During the final quarter of the twentieth century the debate over both the ethics and the efficacy of zoos became more heated. Supporters argued that it wasn't practical or possible to study animals up close in the wild, and zookeepers posited that they provided the ideal setting for research, as well as for maintaining the diversity of species and educating the public about the issue. Zoos also became more spacious and humane in their treatment of their inhabitants, and curators sought to prove that the animals were actually happier in a predator-free environment. Critics countered that zoos were mostly interested in improving husbandry, that any research they conducted could study only abnormal behaviors adopted in unnatural settings, and that they bred only the most docile individuals, thus eliminating the naturally aggressive behaviors needed for survival in the wild—traits actually of greater interest to the scientific community.

The best zoological attractions, such as the Zurich Zoo, the Woodland Park Zoo in Seattle, and to some extent the Arizona-Sonora Desert Museum outside Tucson, were becoming bioparks, which integrated animals and plants from land and water into environmental centers. The critics continue, however, to charge that even the best facilities distort animal behavior and that research on the animals is therefore at least partially invalid. Zoos, they say, divert public funding and attention from the preservation of natural habitat and are inescapably unethical as they keep animals prisoner for our pleasure. Hence the PETA demonstrators outside the door today.

There seems little doubt that Fischbacher and Horn care as deeply about their cats as does Wynn about his art. And it seems likely, since they loan animals to zoos and help fund conservation efforts for Asian tigers, that they believe they are, at a minimum, offsetting any harm they may be causing the biosphere with their entertainment business. Sincerity is not the issue in my mind. What gives me pause is that the rhetorical ground seems to be shifting once again.

Zoos are now breeding what they know to be genetically inferior species, such as Cincinnati with its white tigers and the Johannesburg Zoo with its white lions. The last pride of wild white lions was seen in South Africa near Kruger Park, and the Pretoria Zoo obtained three of them in 1975 with hopes of preserving the strain. The Pretoria, also known as the National Zoological Garden of South Africa, was founded in 1899 and is considered one of the best zoos in the world. As part of its normal operating procedures, it shared some white lion cubs with its sister zoo in Johannesburg. In 1994 the zoos in South Africa were told that they could no longer rely on state subsidies and would have to raise much more of their own income. The Jo'burg zoo then lent out males with the requisite recessive genes to a breeder, who would sell the cubs to interested parties and donate half the profits to the zoo. (The Johannesburg Zoo, in fact, is where Siegfried and Roy obtained their white lions, in 1996 the first ones to be brought into the United States.)

Zoos do not breed animals for hunting, but once the cat is out of the bag . . . Within a year or two, white lions were being advertised on Internet hunting sites, and in 2003 there were fifty-two known white lions at four breeding sites in South Africa serving a market of nine thousand game ranches. Some of the ranches are so small that an animal has no place to elude the hunters. This kind of exploitation is partly an indirect consequence of zoo administrators' treating animals as assets generating revenue through attendance and licensing fees, an objectification of their status that makes them comparable to the artworks in museums.

I have no illusions about people giving up the right to purchase animals from zoos, breeders, or poachers in the wild to keep as pets. William Randolph Hearst had the largest private zoo in the world at his San Simeon castle, including everything from Asian and African antelope to yaks, lions, leopards, and a cheetah—three hundred animals in all. Getty followed suit with menageries at both his Malibu properties and at Sutton Place in England. Both men were simply doing what the rich and powerful have always done, collecting what interested them.

Nor do I spend time wishing that zoos will free their subjects—because despite their critics, zoos do manage to preserve bits and pieces of the planet's gene pool, and they do educate the public. As Hancocks points out, psychological studies on the attitudes of zoo visitors show that badly designed zoos where the animals are kept in inappropriate surroundings (in solitude, in cramped enclosures, on too much concrete, and with nothing natural to play with) can actually negatively impact people's ideas about the value of wildlife and increase their feelings of dominion over the natural world. But when captive animals are placed in ample environments with other species and given opportunities for privacy so that the visitor is not in complete control of the viewing, they are seen as being more important than their keepers and onlookers. In such settings, often designed as immersive landscapes extending seamlessly from viewing area to habitat, the animals are seen (or not seen) more on their own terms, and visitors may remember that nature is not always under the thumb of culture—their experience tends more toward awe and reverence. Clearly, given the reaction of the two girls in front of the black panther cage, the Secret Garden and its overlords are far from achieving that standard, as Roy Horn was reminded so forcibly in front of his audience.

SHARKS IN THE SAND

The opulence of the Secret Garden, which returfs the lion and tiger cages every twenty-four hours, and its presentation of nature
as yet another experience to be consumed as spectacle contrasts
severely with the Southern Nevada Zoological-Botanical Park,
otherwise known as the Las Vegas Zoo, a dusty three acres located
in North Las Vegas on the edge of a suburb. As I pull up next to the
chain-link fence that surrounds the facility, three peafowl are
pecking around in the dirt; when I open the car door they strut
unhurriedly back through a gap in the mesh. The muffled roar
of a lion echoes across the street and out among the one-story
ranch-style houses of the neighborhood. The boundary between
the zoo and the citizens here, while perfectly safe, is more permeable than at the Secret Garden, where access to the wildlife is
mediated by the resort's massive walls.

Pat Dingle, the director, welcomes me into his office, lights a
cigarette, and leans back in his chair before sketching out a history

of the zoo. A lean, tanned man in his fifties, he speaks with a care and courtesy that betray the years he spent in the navy as a radarman during Vietnam and then as a detective with the local police department. He resigned as a senior detective when he was thirty-two, already in the thrall of a lifelong passion for breeding rare birds, a hobby that had led him to open his own store and eventually become friends with the curator of birds at the San Diego Zoo. In 1980 he started what he intended to be a bird park, then added a petting zoo. This blossomed into a vision for a large desert biopark, and he leased 250 acres of state land in preparation for the attraction, which would have been two and a half times the size of the San Diego Zoo.

The biopark didn't happen, perhaps in part because the city of Las Vegas has never expressed any serious interest in supporting a zoo, which in other cities is often the given means of underwriting. But after all, why should it? Within roughly nine miles of the zoo, almost any resident or visitor can see the lions and tigers of the Bellagio, the lions at the MGM, the tiger and reptile habitats at the Tropicana, the immense tropical aquariums of the Mirage and Caesars Palace, and the state-of-the-art Shark Reef at Mandalay Bay.

Dingle runs his operation on an annual budget of around $400,000 with six full- and part-time employees and strong volunteer support. They are slowly renovating the original 1940s building on the site—appropriately enough for worshippers of nature, it was a church—and expanding the collection of 150 animals and plants through a variety of means. Some of the animals, such as Terry the chimpanzee, are former showbiz performers who became too old and would have otherwise been destroyed. Others, such as a pair of Barbary apes, were loaned from the San Diego Zoo and have since produced offspring. Dingle has otters coming from the national zoo in Ottawa and a Chinese alligator from the Bronx

Zoo. He also has bred the largest collection of rare swamp wallabies in the country and now sells some of them to other zoos.

It's obvious, however, that Dingle is not in this for the money, nor is he interested in pursuing a larger vision. The zoo sees between fifty thousand and sixty thousand visitors a year, as compared with the million-plus paying almost three times as much to visit the Shark Reef at Mandalay Bay. "Las Vegans have a short attention span," Dingle observes drily, "and they don't go out when it's over a hundred degrees or less than forty, or if it's too windy. Their major recreation is slots. Go look at the parking lot of Texas Hotel next door—it's full, and these are locals, not tourists." Dingle is concentrating instead on making the zoo "a diamond," a small attraction designed for a couple of hours of visitation and not for competition with anything on the Strip.

I had last visited the zoo two years earlier, and when Dingle takes me for a stroll around the property, I note the many improvements. Paving stones line more of the paths, the enclosures are larger and more sophisticated, and the plants providing shade and definition to the property are more numerous—and also afford the residents a bit more privacy. At one point we stop by the pen occupied by a juvenile American alligator, who swims over to Pat expecting to be fed. It's an aggressive species that can grow up to twelve feet in length, and Dingle obviously respects its power. It has chased him out of the pen several times during the last few months.

The zoo's twenty-three-year-old Bengal tiger, a seven-and-a-half-foot-long female weighing 280 pounds, is napping in the shade. The Bengal's enclosure is much smaller than that afforded the cats at the Mirage, and yet I don't feel the same degree of dismay as at the resort's facility. Some of it has to do with the vigor of the respective animals. The cats at the Mirage are young, while the Bengal has already lived six years beyond her life expectancy, and I've never seen her as restless as her showbiz counterparts.

Many of the zoos in America started as a convenient way for circuses and other traveling menagerie shows to dump their animals, as well as for more enlightened donations, and the Las Vegas Zoo is no exception. (Neither, for that matter, is the San Diego Zoo, which was founded to house the animals formerly appearing in the 1915 Panama-Pacific Exposition.)

It's also a question of motive. Dingle is running a zoo built around the premise that people should have a chance to gaze deeply and closely into the eyes of the Other, which is a very different matter from putting on a magic show or overwhelming you with big cats. The point of the zoo is to experience the animals themselves, not as a feature pulling in foot traffic in order to increase the bottom line of a hotel-casino.

〰 Pat Dingle says that he never visits attractions on the Strip, but I wonder if he's at least seen the advertisement for Shark Reef that's posted alongside I-15 at the southern end of town. Driving in from L.A. a couple of months earlier to attend the Warhol show at the Bellagio, I passed by a double billboard. One side featured a skimpily clad showgirl sprawled invitingly on her side. On the other half a shark swam toward her feet with its mouth agape, an advertisement for the attraction at Mandalay Bay. "Kill an hour of time," it urged. On this trip the first side features two fetching women bracketing an ad for Escort.com: "Girls direct to your room." The shark's snout now points directly at the derriere of one of the models. I find it revealing that the escort services girls have on more clothes than did the showgirl previously posted.

Robert Hughes could have been talking as much about zoos as about art museums when he proclaimed the impossibility of the latters' competing with the visual attractions of the Strip. Little did he envision the hotel-casinos themselves incorporating art into the visual spectacle of the street. The situation with zoological attractions could be said to have followed the same pattern. Tourists aren't much inclined to visit a local zoo, and in any case the Strip operators simply added their own zoological attractions.

Pat Dingle's operation started as a petting zoo and retains the scale and flavor of that endeavor because the city—meaning, ultimately, the voters—can't see a reason to support anything better. The Las Vegas Natural History Museum started as a taxidermy shop, and although it now occupies a 38,000-square-foot office building donated by the city, it too struggles and is likewise lashed to its past. Although the twelve-year-old organization has a budget and visitation rate in the same range as the zoo, the Web site for *Frommer's Las Vegas 2004* describes it in not exactly kind terms: "This humble temple of taxidermy hearkens back to elementary-school field trips circa 1965, when stuffed elk and brown bears forever protecting their kill were as close as most of us got to exotic animals." Neither the Las Vegas Art Museum nor the Las Vegas Zoo even appears in the guide. None of the three nonprofits—the art museum, the zoo, the natural history site—has been able to rally the community support that other cities with smaller populations and much less profitable commercial bases have managed to provide. Once again, the public has ceded responsibility to the private.

If the Bellagio art gallery was a prelude to the Guggenheim's coming to town, then Wynn's dolphin habitat and lobby aquarium foreshadowed Shark Reef, the only zoological attraction in Nevada accredited by the American Zoo and Aquarium Association. Out of the approximately 16,000 museums in America in 2004, 750 were accredited by the American Association of Museums. The only art museums in Nevada thus accredited were the Guggenheim and the Nevada Museum of Art in Reno. Among other things, the Las Vegas Art Museum lacks not only the security, climate control, and curatorial policies needed in order to win accreditation, but even the staff necessary to undertake the long-range planning that is integral to the three-year process.

On the freeway headed back to the hotel, a brightly adorned minivan passes me. It's a Pink Jeep Tour vehicle loaded with tourists bound for the Red Rock Natural Conservation Area west of town, a 2,500-foot vertical sandstone escarpment whose cliffs rival Yosemite's in size and grandeur. Were it not for the presence of the Strip, the cliffs would be the most noteworthy physical feature of the valley. On the back of the van a sign urges: "See the natural Las Vegas." But in order to do so, the company takes you out of town. There's nature in Las Vegas—from lions and tigers to bare-naked ladies, from African penguins at the Flamingo to twelve-foot nurse sharks at Mandalay Bay—but not much that's natural, to be sure.

I valet park in midafternoon at the back of the resort. You have to walk halfway around the sixty-acre property to get to Shark Reef, a strategy to swing you past the shops and restaurants—but at least you're spared the casino. The first eateries are the Rumjungle, then Red Square with its headless plaster statue of Lenin guarding the front. The doors of the restaurants are open, but no one is inside, a series of empty stages awaiting the theater of the night. The *faux* pigeon-decorated (the droppings are actually paint) statue of the Russian leader is headless because servicemen objected to the intact likeness as symbolic of Communism. Currently the 250-pound head sits in a block of ice that resides in the vodka locker, where sable-draped patrons select $100 bottles to quaff with Beluga caviar. Traipsing deeper into the hotel I pass Aureole, where in the evening harnessed wine stewards zip up and down on wires inside a four-story glass-and-steel wine tower to retrieve your selection from its 9,865 bottles.

As with the dolphin habitat at the Mirage, here I again walk above an enormous swimming pool area before reaching Shark Reef. The eleven-acre water park is planted with palm trees, and its sand-and-surf beach is littered with young women wearing thong bikinis, yet another kind of nature encounter heavily marketed on the Strip. It all serves to enhance the illusion of being at a tropical resort.

At the Shark Reef ticket booths I obtain a press kit and a security escort. Adult admission is $14.95, kids under twelve pay $9.95, and those under four enter free. Reduced rates for residents are available but not specified as to amount. The 105,000-square-foot facility ran around $40 million to construct, so it's not yet had time to earn back its cost, but Francis Béland, the consultant and original director of Shark Reef, told me earlier that the attraction "was originally planned to be a traffic center, not a profit center—but it's exceeded all of Mandalay Bay's goals. It sees more than a million visitors a year and makes a profit." Given the number of people in line to pay, I can believe it.

Beyond the booth double doors open on a foyer with stairs leading up to a thatched tiki hut and a soundtrack of jungle birdcalls. The walls are cast in resin to imitate Mayan stonework, the beginning of the attraction's narrative about a sunken temple slowly being reclaimed by the sea and dangerous predators. The security guard hands me over to the ticket person, who provides me with an audio wand and a pocket-sized print guide that's labeled a "passport" after those used in the national park system. I decline an opportunity to have my picture taken and digitally modified to include one of the glass reef tunnels as a background. And then I descend.

The sloping walkway takes a steady stream of visitors into an atrium filled with both live and artificial foliage, a folded path that accommodates people moving forward and those pausing to view each of the fourteen exhibits, all of which are disguised as mini-habitats. Shark Reef holds more than 2,500 animals of more than a hundred different species, including fifteen kinds of sharks. Its

1.6 million gallons of saltwater are created by mixing dechlorinated local water with a dehydrated seawater called "Red Sea," the whole volume being filtered every thirty to ninety minutes. While the stats from the press kit are striking enough from an engineering standpoint, I'm more impressed by the management of sightlines. I'm never in view of more than twenty or thirty people at a time.

The first exhibit is a pool in which a golden crocodile from Thailand—a pale and beautiful reptile more than six feet long—lounges half in and half out of the water. (I make a note to myself that my choice of verbs risks anthropomorphizing the croc as a lounge lizard.) Unlike the experience at the zoo, there's little reaction or involvement here between the viewers and the viewed. Although this is a rare animal, there's none of the immediacy of seeing Pat Dingle's alligator swim over to him.

Next we work our way down to the aquarium pools, freshwater ones at first, with fish from the Amazon, mostly species I've never seen before, but also the inevitable piranha. Advertising for the attraction is based on putting the public in close proximity with predators, a promise that Shark Reef fulfills—but once you're inside, the rhetoric shifts. The predators are displayed as vulnerable creatures living in endangered ecosystems, and the idea that you're here to witness the grotesque is supplanted by an educational experience. I can't help but think bait-and-switch.

Just before leaving the translucent skylight for the underwater tunnels, we reach the first large seawater tank. Small sharks, moray eels, tropical fish. I try to see to the other end of the pool, but it disappears into the murk, giving me the impression that it continues downward. The path snakes around to the right, doubles back past more reef tanks filled with tropical specimens, then goes left into the first reef tunnel—a transparent tube that runs along the bottom of the tank. You're actually looking up into the first sea-water tank, and I can now see how part of the artificial reef blocks you from seeing either end of the exhibit. The sightlines, like the walkway, are complexly folded to afford the illusion of much more spaciousness than exists in reality. Inside the underwater pedestrian walkway the fake stonework provides a low running bench on either side, and people sit quietly to enjoy the view. It's restful and not at all claustrophobic. People show their kids the fish, listen to their audio guides, or in my case, take notes. We're only ten minutes in, but it's nice to take a break and absorb the visual complexity of the aquarium.

At the far end of the tunnel we leave behind the last of the terrestrial plantings and enter a darkened gallery with multiple displays. A touch tank with rays and horseshoe crabs occupies most of the room. People sit on its rim and put a hand in the water, their fingers grazing lightly across the backs of the rays as they circulate around the edge of the shallow enclosure. Touch pools were featured at the first Sea World in San Diego when it opened in 1964 and have become as common a feature of aquaria as petting zoos are for land-based zoological collections. Both are efforts to bring people "closer to nature," as if our own bodies weren't already animals within touching range.

A young woman whose badge identifies her as a "Naturalist," one of three I see during the tour, sits on the edge of the pool with a microphone. She alternates enticing people to come touch the animals in the water with reminders not to drop purses or cell phones in the tank, and she occasionally answers questions from the audience. Labeling someone who is essentially an usher as a naturalist makes it seem as if we're in a public park and receiving scientific information from a professional scientist. It's a role-playing device used to great effect at places such as Sea World, one meant to reinforce the legitimacy of the entertainment as educa-tion. "Edutainment" is the term some architects have adopted for places such as Sea World.

The San Diego attraction was first planned as an underwater restaurant but was built as a nature theme park when it became obvious that the revenue-generating possibilities for the latter were more lucrative. Currently owned by the world's largest brew-ing company, Anheuser-Busch, there are now nine parks in the chain that draw more than 21 million visitors annually. There is no denying that the parks do employ professional marine biologists, do conduct research and contribute to ocean conservation efforts worldwide, and do offer an educational experience to the public. There is also no denying that the privately owned subsidiary pro-vides environmental coverage for a large and noxious chemical operation, which is what in essence corporate breweries are. The advertised research activities also mask the fact that such com-mercial attractions compete directly with public aquariums for audiences and revenues.

The bottom line for Sea World, as Susan Davis deconstructs it in her book *Spectacular Nature: Corporate Culture and the Sea World Experience*, is measured in attendance figures and revenue, objec-tives also served by science in the form of audience survey statis-tics. The goals for a publicly funded nature attraction, on the other hand, have more to do with increasing public curiosity and knowl-edge about the environment in order to preserve it. Sea World ini-tially positioned itself as an entertainment operation but, during the rising environmental awareness and subsequent federal laws protecting aquatic resources, shifted its image to be an educa-tional one. It is, however, difficult as a visitor to understand the difference between a major zoo, park, or aquarium and a zoological tourist attraction. The rhetoric deployed is remarkably similar, an effective camouflage. Only by noticing how often, for instance, the name "Anheuser-Busch" crops up next to the environmental messages can you sense the corporate strategy—and by comparing the amount of square footage devoted to retail space in a private versus a public aquarium, though the two are moving closer all the time.

In order to take notes, I join the other visitors sitting on the edge of the touch pool, and watch the children approach and gingerly put their fingers in the water as a small ray swims by, making its endless circuits around the perimeter of the shallow enclosure. Stereotypical swimming? I wander over to the small lionfish display nearby. It carries the opposite message of the touch tank: the spines are loaded with a neurotoxin that can give you anything from a severe sting, lasting up to twelve hours, to anaphylactic shock and death. Next to it is another medium-sized reef tank with small leopard sharks cruising around. What most attracts me in the room, however, is a large glass column full of transparent jellyfish, exquisite pulsating flowers that are genuinely alien and mysterious to me. While many people tend to pass by most of the tanks without much pausing, the fuguelike rising and falling of the bell shapes holds them for minutes at a time. It's like watching Chihuly's glass ceiling at Bellagio come alive, although my passport points out that the stinging tentacles of the Australian box jellyfish can kill you within minutes. I suppose standing underneath the two thousand glass flowers during an earthquake could do an even quicker job.

The darkened room, the jellyfish, and the heightened sense of threat provided by the wall labels have led us away from the benign visual theme of a jungle temple sinking into the sea, and serve as a segue into the final room, which evokes a sunken pirate ship. The soundtrack changes too, modulating from jungle birds to creaking timbers and dripping water. In the tunnel that leads into this room, the blue light of an enormous tank flickers around us as we are surrounded by the largest animals we'll see here, including forty sharks. A large nurse shark cruises by, and then the only hammerhead shark in closed captivity, a nightmare on steroids. Despite the prehistoric appearance of the hammerhead, the languorous nurse shark is the species more dangerous to humans. Green sea turtles, moray eels, stingrays, and barracuda undulate in and out of sight. I walk over them on glass, and they swim overhead. Both the transparent acrylic tunnel and the rhetoric about the sharks are virtually identical to Sea World's Shark Encounter.

If any part of the attraction would scare you, this would be it. I've been in open water with these animals — diving with nurse sharks, surfing with hammerheads, snorkeling with barracuda; and I've found myself unexpectedly nose-to-nose with morays and lionfish. Many of those times I was scared half out of my wits. Here the environment is a studied calm, and the audio wands seek to impress the visitor with the fact that humans are hunting sharks into extinction, not vice versa. The threat level for shark attacks is vanishingly low — no matter what the billboard by the freeway suggests.

It's taken me and my cohort of fellow visitors thirty minutes to arrive here, and by this time no one seems anxious, merely curious. Shark Reef has enticed customers with the lure of being in proximity to dangerous and exotic animals, educated us about their habitats and our deleterious effects on them, and given us a visual narrative so dense and handsome that I'm tempted to walk through the entire attraction a second time. I do, in fact, backtrack to the jellyfish in order to reenter the final room, then linger there long after the rest of my group has exited.

The exit from the last tunnel, away from the cool blue-green underwater glow and back into hot sunlight, seems too short. The way out, of course, puts everyone in front of the gift shop with its plush sharks and sea shells, well positioned to take advantage of the faint emotional exile I feel. According to Brian Robison, Shark Reef's current director, 84 percent of the visitors are from out of town and only 16 percent are Las Vegans, a percentage Robison and his staff are trying to increase with special promotions—like their annual tax day, when they have accountants on hand to help you file your federal income tax returns. I think that locals, given the price break, might be tempted to come more than once with their kids, relatives, and friends from out of town.

Francis Béland had told me that the original planning document for the attraction suggested that all comparison with aquariums should be avoided. Shark Reef was designed to be an entertainment that had educational value, not vice versa. However, Shark Reef is managed by the Vancouver Aquarium Marine Science Center, which means that by virtue of both its own internal standards and the external ones of the American Zoo and Aquarium Association, the health of the animals is the first priority. Furthermore, as Robison described to me, Shark Reef maintains a research committee to vet proposals for research, and they conduct original husbandry work.

It's clear that, just as in the art world, where the distinctions between for-profit and not-for-profit operations are increasingly erased, so it is with zoological attractions, the trend made all the more apparent by the enormous amounts of capital available in Las Vegas to push the envelope. Shark Reef doesn't merely look like a functioning aquarium, it is one—another example of how themed tourist attractions approach the reality of civic amenities elsewhere. I have no objection as long as audiences realize that they are being treated as consumers of spectacle, not students of the environment—but the visual rhetoric and signage are meant to disguise that distinction.

〜 Walking back along the corridor elevated above the beach, I look out the windows at the sunbathers, an anonymous voyeur, and feel as if I'm peering into another exhibit. There is very little that is not on display and under continual scrutiny in Las Vegas—including each and every visitor. It's difficult to remember at times that these are not public attractions, but private property under constant surveillance by cameras. When you're inside the Guggenheim at the Venetian, you automatically assume that you're being surveilled—the guards are obvious, of course, and cameras watch over the art. When you walk outside, however, and the ceiling lifts out of sight, it feels as if you're entering a public commons, and you forget that you're still being scanned by several of the more than 1,200 cameras overhead. Many of the closed-circuit TV units can pan, tilt, and zoom down to the serial numbers of a dollar bill held in your hand, and special 360-degree panoramic videos survey the entire floor. Facial-recognition software is used to identify not only known criminals but also high rollers. It's not just the animals that lack privacy in Las Vegas. We've become so blasé about being watched that the NBC network has a television series, *Las Vegas*, about a fictional surveillance team. The show is shot on location here at the hotel.

Hanging in Brian Robison's office is a reproduction of the original painting used to advertise the opening of Shark Reef. The foreground is all red sand, the background formed by the skyline of the Strip. The fin of a shark is plowing ripples through the sand, headed into town. The image both captures the absurdity of putting an aquarium in the desert and plays on the real dangers that lurk in Las Vegas. Two-legged sharks prowl the tables looking for ways to beat the system, and stalk the slot machine aisles looking for unattended purses and pockets; hence the cameras. In the Mandalay's hotel rooms, a live feed from the shark tank is available on your television set. Spectacle, to be effective, has to be threatening at a discernible level so that the audience can at least sense, if not understand, the degree of power deployed to keep it under control. That power is therefore made visible, and even increased, by deliberately exposing the surveillance, whether we're watching the helplessly caged tigers, the closed circuits of the sharks, or a TV show about clandestinely scrutinizing our fellow humans.

FOUNTAINS AND MOUNTAINS

The most severe disjunct in Las Vegas between reality and imagination—which under the particular circumstances of this book
might also be equated to the distance between nature and culture—is reserved for how its inhabitants use water. Las Vegas is
built in the Mojave Desert, the hottest and driest of America's five
deserts, yet it has always used water as the signature of its existence. To understand how surreal the gap is between the Mojave
and Shark Reef—or worse, between the desert and the ubiquitous suburban lawns—a short digression into the local history
and statistics of water is necessary.

The name Las Vegas means "the meadows" in Spanish and
arises from the fact that early explorers found a small wetlands
three miles west of what is now downtown Las Vegas. Its pools were
surrounded by cottonwoods, reeds, and native grasses, the artesian waters upwelling so strongly that it was impossible to sink in
them when swimming. It was a rare and precious oasis in a region

that receives on average only four inches of precipitation annually, and the springs had served as a waypoint for Indians during the ten thousand years of human habitation preceding the invasion of European settlers.

Brigham Young sent a group of Mormons south from Salt Lake City in 1855 with the express mission of colonizing the valley. They successfully used the outflow of the springs to irrigate their crops, but the isolation and astringency of the environment proved too much, and they abandoned the effort after less than three years. For several decades afterward modest ranching was conducted in the valley, and the watering hole continued to serve travelers on their way along the increasingly popular Mormon Trail that stretched from central Utah to Los Angeles. In 1902 the San Pedro, Los Angeles & Salt Lake Railroad purchased the springs from the largest ranch. The water necessary for the steam locomotives was channeled from the springs in redwood pipes to a site near the abandoned Mormon fort. In 1905, upon the opening of regular service, the railroad created the Las Vegas Land and Water Company, platted the surrounding land, and sold lots at auction.

The spring water was supplemented starting in 1907 with nearby groundwater wells, but by 1935 the springs' outflow, Las Vegas Creek, was beginning to run dry during the summer. During a severe water shortage in 1947, residents convinced the state legislature to create the Las Vegas Valley Water District (LVVWD), a government agency that would regulate wells and begin to take advantage of Colorado River water. In 1952 the LVVWD bought the Land and Water Company, and two years later began piping water in from Lake Mead. The springs themselves finally dried up completely in 1962.

Approximately 6,800 local wells now supply 12 percent of the valley's needs, but the groundwater basin feeding them is only about 1,600 square miles in extent—which is to say, primarily the mountains you can see to the city's west and north. The estimated recharge of that basin from precipitation is between 40,000 and 60,000 acre-feet annually (one acre-foot — an acre of water one foot deep — being about what it takes to support a family of four for a year). Las Vegas has since at least 1950 been pumping out groundwater faster than it recharges, which has lowered the water table by three hundred feet, caused the surface of the valley to subside by as much as six feet in places, and in turn ruined residential and business-building foundations in nearby North Las Vegas. Despite conservation measures, pumping is still double or triple the rate of recharge.

The remaining 88 percent of the water used in the Las Vegas area comes from the Colorado River, which the city didn't start tapping for even industrial use until 1942, seven years after the completion of Hoover Dam. By then the river waters had already been divvied up by the Colorado River Compact, a 1922 federal law that allocates the river's total flow among seven states and Mexico. Although Las Vegas has been the fastest-growing metropolitan area in the country since the 1980s, the compact allows Nevada only 300,000 acre-feet annually, the least of any of the eight entities. To make matters worse, the amounts were set according to a formula that was based on the river's volume during an extremely wet period.

The legal entitlements for the river are currently at 17.5 million acre-feet (maf), but the actual average flow during most of the twentieth century was less than 15 maf. Since 2000 the river has been flowing at only 10 maf, due to a record-breaking drought now in its sixth year. Lake Mead, the largest artificial lake in the United States, is down more than 75 feet, and the upstream reservoir of Lake Powell down almost 150. Even though 85 percent of the river's flow is devoted to agriculture in the various states, the estimated population dependent upon the Colorado is 25 million people; that's expected to rise to 38 million no later than 2020. California, the fastest-growing state, is already overdrawing its annual allotment by a million acre-feet.

The average water consumption per day in the United States now runs about 190 gallons per person. In the Mediterranean climate of Los Angeles, where it rains almost fifteen inches per year, it's 140; in Tucson, with rainfall around twelve inches, it's been cut in half in recent years to 160. In profligate Phoenix, which still gets more water from the Colorado than it can use, the rate is 226 gallons per day. Las Vegans, however, use more water than any other urban folks in the country, 307 gallons. Both local government and residents have known for years that the supply of water to Las Vegas had limits that were ever more rapidly being approached. With the drought, that limit basically has been reached for the moment.

Not only is the water use here prodigious and unsustainable, most of it is unnecessary. About 65 percent of water use in the valley is residential, and two-thirds of that is used outside. During the summer as much as 60 percent of all water pumped in the valley is thrown in the air in order to water lawns. The water district estimates that Las Vegans waste as much as 30 billion gallons of water per year, most of it from citizens overwatering their turf, which is why the LVVWD now pays residents a dollar per square foot of turf removed. Taking out one average lawn can save as much as 100,000 gallons per year, almost one-third of an acre-foot.

Las Vegas is currently under a severe drought alert, with curtailed lawn watering and limits on the amount of turf that can be planted around new homes. Even businesses with fountains are fined for running them. The restrictions, however, do not apply to the fountains on the Strip.

〜 With that context in mind, I've decided to return to the Las Vegas Springs Preserve to see what progress is being made on the creation of an ecopark in the middle of the city. I take off from

Robert Beckmann's house in the foothills of Henderson near the far southeastern corner of the valley and drive down into the layer of morning smog pressed down over the city by an inversion, a condition typical in the Basin and Range province of the Interior West. The heavier cold air settles on the valley floors while the warmer air rises, forming a lid that holds in the pollutants. The inversion creates a counterintuitive situation in which the higher you go out of the valley in winter, the warmer it gets.

Each time I drive across the Las Vegas Valley, I detour by the Wynn Las Vegas project. When I came up from Los Angeles in November 2002 to write about the Bellagio art gallery, bull-dozers were still preparing the site. When I passed it eleven months later on my way to visit the Las Vegas Zoo, ten stories of bronze-tinted glass gleamed on the facade of the hotel tower. Now, only two months since, a series of enormous vertical concrete culverts loom in front of the curved facade of the resort, service columns the diameter of my living room meant to carry power and water to the top of the eight-story artificial mountain that Wynn is building, a gigantic berm that will wrap around a series of artificial lagoons. The models show that the mountain will hide the three-acre water feature from the Strip but expose it to the hotel. On the inside different aspects of the landscaping will reveal themselves from various angles, ranging from dramatic waterfalls to a serene facade with a temple. The overt purposes behind putting such a massive earthen wall between the street and the hotel are twofold: to create a sense of mystery and to disguise the scorching aridity of the environment. In theory people will want onto the property in order to see what's behind the mountain, while guests will luxuriate in visual relief from the flat, dry desert.

The idea of piling up massively elevated terrain in the middle of a flatland is, like assembling a menagerie of animals from far-away places, another traditional method of demonstrating wealth and power, of defying the nature of a space while transforming it into an exotic place—or palace. It is also, as Carl Hagenbeck well knew when he built his artificial mountain outside Hamburg, a way of increasing the square footage of your territory within a bounded horizontal footprint by ascending vertically. The size of Wynn's artificial mountain, which will be planted with mature trees, is along the order of the fabled Hanging Gardens of Babylon, which were located thirty miles south of present-day Baghdad. This second of the seven wonders of the world (in terms of date of construction) was a ziggurat of baked mud bricks that has long since disappeared. Legend has it that Nebuchadnezzar II (604–562 BC) built the terraced pyramid in order to pacify his wife, Amyitis, who pined for her green and mountainous homeland of Media but found herself living on the arid and windswept plains of Mesopotamia. According to the Sicilian historian Diodorus Siculus, writing four hundred years later, the garden was four hundred feet square and eighty feet high: "The approach to the Garden sloped like a hillside and the several parts of the structure rose from one another tier on tier. . . . On all this, the earth had been piled . . . and was thickly planted with trees of every kind that, by their great size and other charm, gave pleasure to the beholder. . . . The water machines [raised] the water in great abundance from the river, although no one outside could see it."

The Hanging Gardens were the world's first known theme park—that is, an attraction meant to distract people from reality by representing in miniature another environment for them to enter. Nebuchadnezzar may have constructed the gardens to preserve his arranged marriage, and Wynn is also erecting a seductive monument, one built for the benefit of visitors who will welcome a green oasis in the middle of a plain as arid as Iraq. His strategy of exclosing the aridity from his guests is one Wynn has used before, notably at Shadow Creek, the most luxurious golf course in the valley and one that consistently ranks among the top ten modern courses in America. The 260-acre layout, surrounded by an impenetrable stockade of pine trees, is irrigated with a million gallons of water daily and was designed to evoke Pinehurst, the revered classic course in North Carolina.

A designer who worked on the Shadow Creek facility once told me that a month before the course opened in 1989, Wynn made an inspection tour. I believe the story because it prefigures exactly Wynn's reaction to the Chihuly ceiling at the Bellagio: Wynn wanted his golf course to look more like North Carolina and instructed his people to double the number of trees planted along the fairways. The landscapers spent seven figures but got the job done on time. Wandering among the twenty thousand trees they planted are swans, pheasants, and African cranes — an embellishment somewhat beyond the grounds at Pinehurst.

It is not a trivial matter for the Mirage waterfalls to run five thousand gallons per minute, a prolixity that Wynn will exceed at his new resort, but the juxtaposition of such liquid riches and a place so arid demonstrates conclusively that "money flows uphill toward money," as Marc Reisner put it in *Cadillac Desert: The American West and Its Disappearing Water*. That's a clever assessment framed in a reversal of physics, but there's another counterintuitive inversion to note. What's at issue with the fountains on the Strip is actually not how much water they use, but the symbolism. The water in most of the elaborate displays, save that which is lost through evaporation, is recycled, and the resorts, which in total use only 10 percent of the water in town, waste far less than homeowners do. But the resorts' highly visible display of water, as if it were a captive element made to jump through hoops, is a powerfully symbolic gesture that is a counterincentive to other businesses and residents to conserve the resource.

"Fountain" originally meant spring, and a spring in the desert—an oasis—formed the basis for the earliest known gardens. Water was brought forth in the middle of the garden, then diverted in four streams to the cardinal points of the compass, a design that represented the subjugation of the resource for agriculture. This was an early instance of demonstrating through symbolic means that humans were in control of the liquid. In larger gardens the quadrants were further divided and then subdivided into a grid watered by fountains and shaded by trees and pavilions. By 3000 BC the Persians had taken the idea to their outposts in Egypt, then later to India. This was the geometry that informed the foundations laid by Nebuchadnezzar, as well as the modern urban grids of Salt Lake City, Los Angeles, and Las Vegas.

The sixteenth and seventeenth centuries were the golden age of fountains in the West. Once the papacy rebuilt the ancient aqueducts serving Rome, enough water pressure was created to support monumental hydraulic displays, many of which featured neoclassical architecture and statuary. The technology soon found its way to France, and inventors began to engineer water-powered automatons. Classical Rome and Renaissance Europe are among the more predominant architectural motifs of the Strip, so it is no surprise that Caesars has a fountain in its retail Forum Shops modeled after the Trevi in Rome or that the Paris hotel-casino across the street from the Bellagio duplicated the fountain in the Place de la Concorde. One of the Caesars fountains even features animatronic *faux* marble gods that periodically move, an allusion to the earlier automatons.

The Dancing Fountains at the Bellagio, of course, had to outdo everyone else's water features, and its twelve hundred custom jets were invented and built by Water Entertainment Technology, which is headquartered in Universal City. Powered by compressed air, the jets fire seventy-five-gallon bursts of water 250 feet into the air; the dancing streams are axisymmetric laminar flows that are to water what a laser is to light, a coherent and smooth stream. Sitting at the intimate outdoor terrace bar on the lagoon outside Picasso (the Bellagio restaurant decorated with original paintings and ceramics by the artist) and watching the thousand-foot-long curtain of water rise to a Frank Sinatra tune, while across the way the five-hundred-foot half-scale Eiffel Tower is bathed in golden floodlights—it's the most romantic piece of theater in town.

It's not just the architecture and the art from Europe that are being reproduced along the Strip, but the environment as well. When the thousand water jets let off for the finale and several tons of water are suspended 250 feet high in front of you, the humidity rises almost instantly, the temperature drops dramatically, and you feel yourself transported out of the desert heat. For many of the 35 million people visiting Las Vegas every year, it suddenly feels more like the air in Rome, where on average it rains twenty-six inches annually, or like Paris with its twenty-three inches.

Among the many consequences of a net gain of six thousand or more residents a month is that the vast majority arrive from wetter climes, bringing with them a mental landscape that receives more rain than the Mojave Desert. Along with our species's genetic favoritism toward the temperate woodlands and savanna of Africa, those relatively well-watered environments in which we primates evolved over several million years, Americans lug around the cultural misconception —as Steve Wynn well knows—that the world should be landscaped to look like a golf course in North Carolina. That is a sustainable vision only if your front yard receives more than twenty inches of rain a year.

How do you get the homeowners to rip out their sod and replace it with xeriscaping when they see the waterfalls at the Mirage and the Dancing Fountains at Bellagio? Furthermore, if you are Patricia Mulroy, the general manager of the Las Vegas Valley Water District, how do you negotiate with your neighboring states over the use of Colorado River water when the displays on the Strip under-cut your hand?

What you do is recruit the man who built the largest water-based theme attraction in the city, Francis Béland, and put him in charge of a publicly funded, private nonprofit ecopark that can deploy all the entertainment technology of the Strip in your cause. Béland, who is the director of both the Las Vegas Springs Preserve and the foundation that supports it, is thus a dual employee of private and public entities. He is an elegant and articulate thirty-two-year-old who studied in Vancouver to be a marine biologist, got an MBA in tourist management from McGill University in Montreal, and came to Las Vegas in 1999 to direct the construction and staffing of Shark Reef. Béland speaks with just a slight French accent, wears good suits and starched white shirts with an open collar, and although now director of the $180-million Las Vegas Springs Preserve, can't help but continue to refer to Shark Reef in the first person plural, as in "We built. . . ." He displays a continuity of enthusiasm and philosophy between the private and public sectors, an admirable and necessary quality for someone hired to manage what is classi-fied in policy circles as a "quango," or quasi-autonomous nongov-ernmental organization.

The Las Vegas Springs, the original fountain of the valley, formed a mound that still exists—the Plymouth Rock of the community, as people at the preserve point out. Historical photographs show Indians still using its waters at the turn of the last century, and in 1972 archeological surveys were begun by a UNLV anthropologist, Claude Warren, who established that people had been using the springs for thousands of years. The LVVWD then petitioned to have the site listed in the National Register of Historic Places, a status granted in 1978. As the agency modernized the artesian wells on the site, it continued to assess the unique natural and cultural heri-tage of the riparian and desert shrub habitats. In 1990 two rare plant species, the Las Vegas bearpoppy and white bearpoppy, were identified, and in 1997 a cooperative management plan guaranteed that the district would protect them. The following year the foundation was established in order to preserve the site and its resources. The archeological and bearpoppy sites were marked off for protection, and historical structures, such as the springhouse and derricks, were stabilized and then rehabilitated as necessary. The foreign tamarisks, also known as saltcedar, were cleared out and the ground reshaped for what will be the most advanced public water education facility in the country.

These changes, as profound as they were, were mostly invisible to passersby on the US 95 expressway to the north. They are even more so with the construction of a "sound wall," a four-thousand-foot-long, thirty-inch-thick stack of compressed hay bales sandwiched between concrete and stucco that runs from sixteen to twenty-one feet high. The hay, specially baled and compressed for construction purposes, is inexpensive, strong, has a high insulation factor, and is accepted as a construction material that meets or exceeds building code requirements for homes. Jesse Davis, a former journalist who now works at the preserve, notes that the wall stays much cooler than regular concrete—by as much as forty degrees on hot days—thus helping to preserve the riparian microclimate inside. The long wall is part of the preserve's effort to demonstrate and promote responsible building techniques.

I take the expressway west from the Strip until the wall, with its colorful water and sun motifs, ends at Valley View, then exit south. On my right is the Meadows shopping mall, which opened in 1978; its hypergreen lawns and shade trees are a landscape aesthetic as out of place in Las Vegas as a xeriscaped cactus garden would be in Boston. To my left is the entrance to the 180-acre preserve. The driveway leads to a parking lot laid atop a huge underground water tank. When construction is complete, visitors will walk from the lot down a *faux* red sandstone wash planted with native shrubs and out onto an orientation plaza, where they can make choices about how to proceed. One option will be the visitors' center with interactive multimedia theaters and galleries that trace the history of water in Las Vegas and display and interpret the natural history of the Mojave.

Another choice will be the waterworks, including the actual pumphouse. Jesse Davis takes me inside the still-unfinished structure. The entrance is an enormous concrete culvert that immediately conveys the scale of the enterprise. The new two-story station will soon control the flow and distribution of the groundwater from the nearby artesian wells. Today its raw concrete walls reverberate with a slow clanging as a workman on the floor below bangs on a white pipe the diameter of a refrigerator, wielding a short sledgehammer to persuade one section to mate with another. Davis grins and guides me over to a series of thick glass windows set into the south wall. He's obviously anticipating my reaction with some pleasure. I press my face against the cool pane and peer into the subterranean gloom beneath the parking lot. Thick columns recede into darkness, and I feel as if I'd discovered a sunken temple—a feeling not unlike that of being at Shark Reef, come to think of it, except that this isn't a simulacrum but a functioning piece of hardware, the interior of the 20-million-gallon tank. Its floor is larger than a football field.

Davis leads me up and out of the building to a white lvvwd pickup truck, whereupon we proceed to tour the grounds. To our east is the Cienega, or wetland, a forty-acre depression originally constructed as a flood-retention basin. It's the central feature of the property and is bordered on one side by a concrete drainage channel. "The Cienega will still function as part of the flood control system, and it's designed to handle two hundred-year floods back-to-back," comments Davis. But now it will also serve as a small wetland for native species and as an educational exhibit circumlocuted by a nature trail.

We drive over to the sound wall, passing along the way huge cottonwoods planted by the Mormons, then park and walk down to the original 1917 springhouse, which has been painstakingly restored. Elms and willows inhabit the riparian section below us, while the higher and drier areas by the ancient spring mound are covered by creosote, sage, tumbleweed, mesquite, and yucca. The foliage provides habitat for more than a hundred species of birds, ranging from hummingbirds to peregrine falcons. Coyotes and foxes still stalk gophers, mice, and squirrels in the preserve. Although the area is too small to support breeding populations of the urban predators, they continue to use it as part of their foraging territory.

I remember how, driving past the preserve before the wall was built, I used to wonder who owned the place. I could glimpse one or two of the wooden derricks built in the early 1940s, but foliage screened most of the structures and the contemporary pumping apparatus. The place was dense with invisible history and life, but because it had not been suburbanized, it looked deserted compared with the shopping mall across the street.

Circling back toward the new pumphouse, we pass the site to be occupied by the Nevada State Museum and Historical Society, which to the perpetual frustration of staff and residents is currently located in Lorenzi Park. The park, which dates from 1921, is another of those anachronistic landscape designs with enormous lawns baking under the sun and lakes that are nothing more than evaporation ponds, complete with fountains to hasten the process. The museum has an extensive collection of local artifacts and mounts exhibitions that are at times excellent, but it suffers from a low visitation rate. The relocation will cure the shortage of visitors, but just as important, it will signal that the public agencies governing Las Vegas finally get it: the past, present, and future of southern Nevada is all about water.

In the modular buildings that serve as temporary offices for Béland and his staff, I spend some time with the balsa model provided by the local architectural firm Tate Snyder Kimsey, which also worked on the West Sahara Library where the art museum is located. The firm specializes in designing institutional structures, including the D Terminal at McCarran International Airport with its playful allusions to early Strip signage and neon. The architects are practiced at integrating local history and geography into their buildings, and the Las Vegas Springs Preserve is no exception. The facility is emphatically not a theme park, but a park that has been themed—the difference being that the former has profit as its goal, while at the preserve the bottom line is learning: everything is aimed at imparting an understanding of the whys and wherefores of water. It is an educational facility wrapped around a working facility, and it uses entertainment technology, such as theme architecture in the artificial wash, to accomplish its goals.

As Béland tells me, "No one tells us how to live here. As a result, we re-create where we come from." One job of the park is to change that: to shift residents from modifying the landscape to modifying their notions of what is appropriate and aesthetic in the desert. This is no small task, given that our notions of beauty in landscape are based genetically in a survival code that tells us that the streams, grasses, and trees of the temperate savanna are the ideal habitat. Béland has focused everything on moving our minds beyond dreams of replicating this ideal environment to an acceptance of local realities. His goal is the opposite of that proposed by the Bellagio, even as he co-opts some of its construction materials and techniques and its visitor philosophy, such as flow from one center of visual attraction to the next in the park. Béland and Mulroy are proselytizing the view that nature is not an experience we can ultimately control, and that we must acknowledge that it controls us. But in order to make the point in the hyperreality of Las Vegas, they are forced to adopt the visual rhetoric of the Strip itself. So, through interpretive materials and the design of the facility itself as part of the educational process, they have made transparent how the preserve's buildings are constructed. They make sure that people will see how the visitor center uses regional, durable, and low-maintenance materials, such as native stone walls, and energy-efficient glass. A demonstration garden nearby will not only exhibit xeriscapes but also teach visitors how to plant them. The retail store will carry books on natural history and sustainable building and landscaping practices. And there is room in the buildings set aside for nonprofit partners, such as the Nature Conservancy.

The growth of Las Vegas isn't about to stop soon, and the auctions that began in 1905 continue. As the valley fills from rim to rim, developers bid to purchase the remaining available public lands from the Bureau of Land Management. The unique arrangement—a compromise worked out initially to preserve the threatened desert tortoise as Las Vegas sought to expand—enables the bureau to use the millions raised each year to buy environmentally sensitive habitat, set aside open lands elsewhere for wilderness (mostly in terrain too steep for the developers to use), and build parks. The policy is, of course, double-edged, preserving habitat while allowing the developers to fill every flat spot in the valley and surrounding lands. The only hope for having enough water is to concentrate not so much on locating more supply (although Mulroy has her eye on agricultural waters in the counties to the north) as on controlling demand.

As far as I can determine, there is no other comparable project in the United States, an ecopark that so thoroughly combines cultural and scientific exhibitions and programs in a matrix of governmental, business, and nonprofit operations. Béland sees the projected 750,000 or so annual visitors to the preserve as including very substantial numbers of tourists from out of town, in particular return visitors seeking new experiences. His ambition isn't just to serve locals but to provide an international educational resource, and that puts his mission on par with that of a major museum. It is logical, I think, that it would be in Las Vegas, where the extreme environment both makes possible and demands imagination, that such an innovative solution would first arise.

The Las Vegas Springs Preserve is a rare instance of technology in a themed environment being deployed in the opposite direction to that taken by the Strip resorts. The hotel-casinos use architectural fantasy and the imprisonment of nature as a way of demonstrating the power of humankind to transcend time and space in the short term. Béland and his colleagues are using it to show the necessity of living within the means dictated by the reality of the here and now.

8

ZUMANITY

Before taking in Cirque du Soleil's new cabaret theater at New York–New York, home of the Canadian-based troupe's *Zumanity* show, Karen and I take a walk through the lobby of the MGM Hotel across the street in order to check out the lions, visible to one and all in their glass enclosures. Five of the big cats are sprawled out, walking, or playing with one of the keepers. A Shark Reef–style transparent tunnel, constructed of inch-and-a-half glass, leads into the center of the small attraction, and a five-hundred-pound male lion walks overhead, much to the amazement of the pedestrians inside. It's a revealing phrase of visual rhetoric, putting sharks and lions literally on top of people, a demonstration of how the food chain works in nature, if not in a hotel. It's also another clever bit of folded topography that increases the space literally and visually. Karen finds the scene even more distressing than the Secret Garden with its big cats. At least there the animals have some distance between them and the gawking humans. The MGM experience is totally invasive, there being no chance for the lions to evade our gaze.

As the Los Angeles writer Ralph Rugoff points out, culture and nature are not two forces opposed to each other, but different points along a spectrum of reality that shift in relation to each other over time and circumstances. A popular image from Las Vegas used to be that of the topless showgirl walking across the stage in high heels with the ostrich feathers on her six-foot-high headdress swaying from side to side. "Ponies" they were called, the tall, small-breasted nudes needed to carry off the look. Five-eight, five-ten, maybe even six feet tall, with long legs and strong backs. It also helped you to keep your balance while wearing fifteen pounds of feathers on your head if you had a background in ballet as a kid.

In the early days of working with tigers in their act, Siegfried and Roy used to turn a young woman into one of the animals, a tidy metaphor for how their routine sublimated the sexy show-girl revues on the Strip into a magic act: exotic women transmuted into exotic cats. When Karen and I went to the Mirage to see the tigers, one of the protesters had a sign that read "Showgirls: Yes. Exotic Animals: No." The conjunction of sex and animals remains ubiquitous in our culture—think how fur coats are advertised in fashion magazines, for example—but never more so than in Las Vegas.

That transmutation of adult desires into family-rated shows lasted about a decade on the Strip. Now sex is back, the over-whelming customer demographic being middle-aged white males who are more interested in escaping child care than in bringing it with them to Las Vegas. The duel between pirate ships in Buc-caneer Bay out front of the Treasure Island, which was a G-rated entertainment alluding to the Robert Louis Stevenson novel, now features lusty young ladies instead of uniformed Royal Navy lads firing cannon at rogues of the Caribbean, and the hotel has been rebranded as the "T.I.," lessening the dependency on the family theme. Now we're back to skimpy costumes and choreography, though the dance has changed.

The detour into family entertainment was started by Jay Sarno. Soon after opening Caesars, he was hard at work implementing the next step in the presentation of fantasy on the Strip, a casino that wasn't just themed around a circus but was the real thing. Circus Circus opened its pink-and-white big top at the north end of the Strip in 1968, two years after Caesars. It was then and remains today the world's largest permanent circus, and featured high-wire acts, jugglers, elephants, and a carnival midway with hawkers luring patrons into traditional "games of chance and skill." Later an arcade was added with two hundred electronic games for both adults and their children. Sarno had brought to Las Vegas not only affordable sybaritic luxury but also the first family-oriented casino, a lesson not lost on Steve Wynn.

The casino did poorly during its first few years, charging what in Las Vegas was a rarity, an entrance fee, and not having a hotel attached to feed customers in the door. Sarno and his partner were bought out in 1974 by Bill Bennett and Bill Pennington, who promptly added a hotel, focused on the profitability of slot machines, and advertised heavily on radio to the middle-class walk-in traffic looking for a bargain vacation without a reservation. Circus Circus soon became one of the most profitable operations in the state. The corporation opened another low-end attraction in 1990, the four-thousand-room Excalibur, an Arthurian castle that held hourly jousts on horseback. Bennett opened the Egyptian-themed Luxor three years later, attempting to diversify the company's offerings with a more upscale property. The effort took some tweaking, and Bennett was forced out of the company during the process, but by then the Circus Circus Corporation was Nevada's largest employer, with eighteen thousand people working for it. In

1999 the company's flagship enterprise, the very upscale Mandalay Bay, opened and the company changed its name from Circus Circus to that of the newest property.

Circus Circus is still going strong, but Mandalay Bay, with its Red Square vodka bar, is very much an adult environment. The proliferation of velvet-roped ultralounges and metaclubs constitutes what Pat Dingle labels the newest fad on the Strip. Light, Ice, Tabu, and the revamped Studio 54 at the MGM, among others, all feature ads in which the young and intensely beautiful "customers" are clothed and acting, not so much as if they're in a nightclub, but as if they're in a nightclub scene from a movie. And that's the point of *Zumanity*. Not to make you feel as if you're in the Berlin of 1932, but as if you're an extra in the movie *Cabaret*.

As one of the interior designers for the major resorts pointed out to me, Las Vegas is all about making you feel as if you're God, which in our imaginations we more often than not compare to being the director of our own movie. You're provided the illusion that you're in control of the climate, the time of day, and—with the dice in your hands—even your own destiny. Being able to access sexual experiences at a variety of levels—from simple voyeurism at topless revues to "escorts" delivered to your room—is essential to maintaining the illusion. It's not that the combination is new; from the moment that the railroad platted the town in 1905 and sold lots, there was a red light district in Las Vegas that offered both gambling and sex. But the scale and depth of the illusion have grown considerably. What is true for the casinos is true for the strip clubs, and what used to be dark, smoke-filled joints with a few girls grinding away around a pole have morphed into luxury palaces such as Sapphire and Treasures.

The former, which cost $25 million to build, is a contemporary black hole of a facility with stars piercing the deep blue backdrop behind the dancers. Patrons can sit at the dim bar and simply watch or, for $20, have a lap dance in a private booth. At 71,000 square feet, Sapphire is the largest topless club in the country, with as many as three hundred dancers performing on a single night, and features sky boxes above the main floor for VIP parties. Treasures looks like—well, the illegitimate child of a bordello and a Greco-Roman bathhouse conceived of by a couple of Texan businessmen—which is pretty much what it is. The brothers Ali and Hassan Davari, who own multiple strip clubs in Houston, built a facility only a third the size of Sapphire but spent $30 million. Marble accents, spotlit custom paintings and statues of nudes, Klimt-like carpets woven in Germany, and private party rooms with their own stages are some of the reasons for the cost. The club also features a surprisingly good restaurant and a decent small buffet. The stage offers state-of-the-art sound and lighting and is flanked by two large glass shower stalls. Use your imagination.

The topless and all-nude clubs are the single most-cited reason visitors give for leaving the premises of the resorts. As Jack Sheehan wrote in the October 2003 issue of *Las Vegas Life*, which was devoted to the topic of "Sex and Sin City," an estimated fifteen thousand exotic dancers work in town, providing a million lap dances a year; the Las Vegas Dancers Alliance estimates that patrons spend $25 million on them annually, a figure growing with the advent of the new clubs. (These figures are estimated to pale in comparison with the hundreds of millions of dollars that escort services and prostitution earn, even though the latter is illegal in Clark County.) While the Guggenheim Las Vegas was drawing a little more than six hundred people per day before it closed the motorcycle show, about fifteen hundred customers crowded Sapphire on a typical Saturday night. The hotels have been eyeing the revenue lost to the strip clubs and wondering how they can recapture it. An obvious answer is to bring the allure, if not the actual performance, of the lap dances into the hotels themselves. *Zumanity*, a show billed as a celebration of human sexuality in all its many guises, is apparently still a work-in-progress and a possible precursor for a Cirque nightclub based around the concept. Presumably that would be a way of keeping more of the adult males in the house.

The idea of an interactive theater themed around a cabaret is an intriguing one that hearkens back to the roots of the French word, which originally meant an establishment serving liquor, then a series of informal salons in late-nineteenth-century Paris where artists and performers would try out their new material in front of a crowd. Le Chat Noir, for example, founded in the Montmartre district in 1881, was frequented by composers such as Claude Debussy and Erik Satie and the writer Guy de Maupassant. By the early 1930s in Weimar Germany, the setting for the 1972 Bob Fosse film *Cabaret*, the gatherings had become intimate clubs where performers routinely transgressed conventional artistic and social boundaries by mingling among, interacting with, and increasingly titillating audience members as they ate and drank at café tables.

~~~ At New York–New York, Karen and I pick up our tickets for the Cirque show and wander into the lobby of the $35-million theater. Its curvilinear walls, stairs, and accents suggest voluptuous female nudes. The wall separating the lobby from the 1,259-seat theater is covered in a plush fabric with peepholes set asymmetrically in it. I press up against the soft barrier to take a look. A wickedly made-up eye zooms in to gaze back at me while heavy breathing plays in my ear, a wordless invitation to enter the showroom.

I have been going to Cirque shows since the mid-1990s and have found them a more astonishing entertainment than almost any other form of theater or dance. The troupe started in 1982 as a group of street performers, Le Club des Talons Hauts (the High-Heels Club), working in Quebec. They obtained financial support from the Quebec government in 1984 to form Cirque du Soleil as part of a national historical celebration, and by 1987–88 they were touring the United States from coast to coast. They first appeared in Las Vegas at the Mirage in 1992 for a year-long engagement, the next year signing a ten-year contract with Steve Wynn to perform *Mystère*. Wynn was so pleased with the results that he built them a $75-million theater for their water-based spectacular *O* at Treasure Island.

A signature aspect of the group's fifteen productions to date is the use of scripts that evoke narrative and character without specifying them. This approach creates a mystery for the audience, a mood that is encouraged by original scores based on relatively exotic musical traditions and played live. You find yourself attempting to create a linear storyline by imagining a relationship from act to act, a very seductive and participatory process that has enticed more than 37 million viewers so far. The anticipation of seeing a new Cirque production is based in no small part on being made to feel as if you're about to enter a whimsical dream with a slightly dark edge—a dream you do more than simply witness, but help create.

Karen makes her living as the house manager of a large nonprofit theater, and as we enter she notes that the ushers, wearing black t-shirts overprinted with seminaked people wearing black thongs and bras, are comfortable moving around the room, a good sign that the show has been well rehearsed. We're seated in the fifth row, and shortly thereafter a slightly cadaverous piano player with long dark tresses saunters onstage, sits at a grand piano, and lights a cigarette before running his fingers slowly over the keyboard. He plies a vampish chanteuse with some mood music while a gigolo wanders the aisle between the stage and audience, lewdly teasing both women and men. A very amply endowed woman with a platter of chocolate-dipped strawberries circulates through the rows of soft red velour seats. She slips adroitly into ours, her alarming fishnet-covered buttocks wiggling past my nose before she turns to offer the sweets. As she hangs vertiginously over my head, her obvious good humor alleviates somewhat the knowledge that, were her cantilevered bosom to fall on me, I'd be smothered to death before someone could lift her up.

This preshow is a narrative frame for the supposedly decadent cabaret that is to follow, a counterpart to the physical frame provided by the design of the theater itself. The architectural curves of the room are, as outside, modeled after the body parts of a woman, the stage a womb and the twin spiral metal staircases on either side of the stage meant to evoke fallopian tubes. Karen points out to me that the carpet is a repeating pattern of abstracted nudes, which turn out to have been based on those in the voluptuous 1862 painting by Jean Auguste Dominique Ingres, *The Turkish Bath*. The images were digitally tweaked to make them deliberately difficult to assemble visually if you're seated on the ground floor, lest any patrons be insulted by walking on unclad female bodies, but from the balcony the forms are more obvious, as we later confirm. The palette of the carpet, the seats, the costumes, the red snakeskin curtain—all of it evokes the lipstick nightlife of 1930s Berlin, a historical reality that most people only know thirdhand through the Fosse film.

No sooner has the temptress finished passing out her strawberries than the band starts playing. As with other Cirque productions, the musicians are visible high above each side of the stage and the score is a world mix that manages to incorporate both frenzied gypsy melodies and seductive Middle Eastern dances. After a skit with a group of confused Puritans, which turns out to be a feeble joke running in between the fourteen acts, and an introduction of the cast by a leather-clad transvestite, an African dance number cranks up the heat. The dancers and the insistent rhythms do a fine job of evoking the entwined roots of dance and sexuality, even if it is a cliché, the use of African dance a signal in our culture that we're being led back to our primal roots.

It was Havelock Ellis, the early-twentieth-century sexologist, who, in his 1923 book *The Dance of Life,* made popular the idea that all dance was based on the courtship behavior of animals from insects to birds to apes. He thought African dance, because it used the entire body, was the most fully realized erotic performance — and that all dance, no matter how aestheticized it became, maintained the connection. Dionysus, the Greek patron of dance, was also the god of fertility and wine, and dates back to pagan roots on Crete circa 3000 BC. Greek dances pantomiming sex survived into Roman times, then made their way into the theater of the Middle Ages and thence into court entertainments.

Although the more formal Western European court dancing had already begun to drift by the 1580s toward narrative ballet, dances from the Middle East had also been making their way via the Moors up through Spain. The *sarabanda*, a group dance performed by women, featured undulating bellies, bawdy songs, and flirtation with the audience, and was also performed at court. Belly dancing from Egypt and Persia, as well as performances based on the legendary biblical "Dance of the Seven Veils" performed by Salome in the first century AD, were popular with court and town alike. Ancient Egyptian art depicts women dancers kicking their heels above the heads of the audience, an early version of what in France would become known as the can-can (originally a French word for "scandal"). The latter, with its girls showing a bit of leg between stockings and underwear, is often cited as the beginning of public nudity in popular dance. By the 1840s the risqué line dancing was incorporated into musical revues; a little over a century later it would surface in Las Vegas with the "Folies Bergere" show at the Tropicana.

～ The next *Zumanity* act takes place in a glass, a very large five-hundred-gallon champagne glass about three feet deep into which two topless Russian women do backflips, entwining with each other in a miniature water ballet that evokes a nostalgia in me for the Glass Pool Inn, which closed just this week. Patrons of the forty-eight-unit motel, which opened in 1952 under the name of the Mirage and built its signature attraction in 1955, could sit around the terrace sipping daiquiris while watching bikini-clad girls through portholes in the sides of the ground-level pool. *Zumanity*'s version is infinitely more acrobatic than anything seen at the motel on the south end of Las Vegas Boulevard, and its choreography is daring, sensual, and tender.

As the show goes on, things become harder edged. About halfway through, Laurence Jardin, costumed in a very nude body stocking, winds herself up off the stage with four black ropes, the only soundtrack her increasingly audible arousal as she works the ropes between her legs. She climaxes high above the audience with a rope wrapped around her throat, a skillful counterfeit of autoerotic asphyxia. Because there's no emotional narrative, however, the act leaves us uninvolved — more a curiosity than a tragic act of snuff-sex.

The most successful of the fourteen acts is "Tissus," a duet with the stunning Olga Vershinina and the muscular blond dwarf Alan Jones Silva. His longing for her onstage is made palpable with credible pantomime, and when she ascends in her white costume by winding herself up a flowing loop of cloth — at first tantalizingly just out of reach, and then higher and higher — the audience audibly bemoans his loss and despair. The narrative is never addressed with words, the relationship between the two never clarified, and at last there's a touch of the trademark Cirque mystery that begs to be unraveled. When Vershinina brings him up to join her, we celebrate not just their erotic fulfillment but an emotional one as well.

That turns out to be the high point of the show. The fifty performers, who range from the endo- to ectomorphic body styles, end up mock-coupling in every combination possible—old to young, large to little, black to white, male to male, female to female—but it feels as if it's a ninety-minute-long catalog of simulated sex set to music. At the end, as we're walking out of the theater, Karen and I agree that the show needs to be far more experimental. Because Cirque is limited by law, if not good taste, as to what it can present onstage in terms of sex and skin, it would seem that a greater use of the surreal—of juxtaposing what seems to be normal and real with that which is unexpected and impossible—would be a good idea.

Robert Beckmann is fond of saying that Las Vegas runs on *frisson*, the sparks that fly off when two things previously not in proximity rub up against each other. Put New York next to Paris next to Venice next to the Mojave and you have *frisson* at several levels, counterposing culture to culture to nature in ways unimagined beforehand. Surrealism likewise depends upon the juxtaposition of unrelated items and conditions—Salvador Dali's melting watches and René Magritte's locomotive steaming out of a fireplace being two examples. (Magritte has been, in fact, an important source of imagery for some of the other Cirque productions, his trademark men in black bowlers one of the company's standard characters thrust into the strange events onstage.) To put it another way, we're used to seeing sex and acrobatics in Las Vegas, and it will take a great deal more of the mysterious to entrance us.

〜 The publicly funded group of street performers that started Cirque du Soleil has now grown into an international corporation. Employing 2,500 people involved in eight productions seen by an estimated seven million people, in 2003 it grossed more than $500 million. This is a prime example of exchange between the nonprofit arts and for-profit entertainment worlds. Artists of all kinds, but in particular performing ones, have always moved between the two, if for no other reason than economic necessity. Performers are more often than not independent contractors and have to take paying gigs where they can find them, whether it's as a violinist for a nonprofit orchestra who does studio work for commercials in Los Angeles or a "legitimate theater" actress accepting a part in a movie. Failure to accept such jobs, assuming you're talented and fortunate enough to be offered them in the first place, can mean flipping burgers for a living. The boundaries in dance are even more permeable because the direct and indirect allusions to sex increase the financial motive.

Ballet (from the Italian *ballare*, to dance) is generally said to have arisen from the court entertainments of the Italian Renaissance in the early 1500s, which often combined music, dance, singing, and recitation during banquets. Catherine de' Medici kept an Italian dance master at the French court, and in 1581 he composed what is considered to be the first ballet, a five-hour-long narrative celebration of the marriage of Marguerite de Lorraine to the Duc de Joyeuse that was also a spectacle celebrating the rites of courtship in general. Audiences sat above the floor in side galleries, a precursor to dance being presented in proscenium theaters in the next century.

The world's oldest ballet company is the Paris Opera, founded in 1669 by Louis XIV, and theatrical ballet consisted of male dancers until the advent of the first ballerina in 1681. Although the men were costumed in tights, the first women in ballet dressed modestly in long hoop dresses. But enjoyment of ballet increasingly depended on being able to watch the dancers' feet and to admire their ability to loosen the bounds of gravity—yet another way of transcending time and space. The Swedish-born French choreographer Charles Didelot, who invented a rigging system of wires to fly ballerinas onstage in 1796, was also the man who put them in tights so we could more readily admire their legs and feet. His rigging also allowed the women to dance *en pointe*. The subsequent development of special pointe shoes made this difficult task more doable, and in 1832 the first great star of the Romantic period in ballet, Marie Taglioni, became the first ballerina to dance consistently on her toes without the aid of wires.

Taglioni helped create a public worship of ballerinas as highly fetishized sex objects—fans began to drink champagne out of used ballet slippers, even roasting and eating them, and ballerinas were sought after as desirable mistresses by wealthy male patrons. Impoverished families saw the ballet as a way for their daughters to rise in social station and made arrangements with dance companies to encourage liaisons. An uncomfortable echo of that practice recently surfaced with several contemporary American dance companies finding yet another way to supplement their revenues by auctioning off their principal dancers for a season. Sponsors pay up to $100,000 for the privilege of supporting a prima ballerina or her partner. No sexual favors are exchanged, nor does the money directly pay the dancer's salary, but some company managers encourage sponsors to visit "their" dancers backstage and entertain them at home.

In the 1860s Edgar Degas began to paint the girls of the corps de ballet, an obsession that would last for more than two decades. Although the artist remained unmarried his entire life and may not have had anything overtly sexual in mind, his sketches captured the relationship between the Paris ballerinas and their older admirers quite accurately. His pictures of seemingly unaware young dancers in vulnerable and awkward poses before mirrors and at the barre carry more than a hint of the voyeur. His bronzes spawned an entire school of semierotic ballet sculpture, often featuring nubile girls with erect nipples, a kitsch aesthetic that still has a market among collectors today.

While the upper and middle classes were appreciating ballet (or at least enjoying being seen in attendance at such an exalted art form), the working people were presented with a form of dance that remained more overtly connected to its roots in sexuality. The Folies-Bergère, the first music hall in Paris, opened in Montmartre in 1869, featuring North African and Oriental-flavored dances that were, in essence, stripteases. Edouard Manet's great painting *A Bar at the Folies-Bergère,* done in 1881–82, is one indication that the artists were there, too, both documenting and making desirable the experience to the cognoscenti.

By the turn of the century Toulouse-Lautrec and Rodin were depicting dancers doing the can-can at the Moulin Rouge. At the same time, Isadora Duncan, who had been born in San Francisco in 1877 and had studied both ballet and burlesque skirt-dancing as a child, was inventing modern dance. Her studies in Greece in 1906 led her to dancing in a simple tunic with her feet bare and her hair loose. Michel Fokine, working for Sergei Diaghilev's Ballets Russes in Moscow, moved past the romantic set pieces of such storybook ballets as *The Sleeping Beauty* and *Swan Lake* and choreographed *Schéhérazade* (1910), a sensual Oriental production featuring Vaslav Nijinsky and other dancers wearing jeweled costumes in an orgy scene, a far cry from the chaste tutus of Paris. Nijinsky took classes from Duncan in 1911 at her Moscow school, which prepared him to star in Paris in the company's daring *L'Après-midi d'un faune* ("The Afternoon of a Faun") in 1912 and then the even more provocative *Le Sacre du printemps* ("The Rite of Spring") in 1913. Sexuality continued to become more openly a theme of the arts during the post–World War I liberalism of France and Germany, and the first nude dancer appeared onstage at the Folies in 1918.

Ballet arrived relatively late in America. Although ballet dancers had lived in and toured the country from the mid-1800s onward and the Chicago Opera had established a small ballet company under its roof in 1910, the first independent American ballet company wasn't established until twenty years after the Sans-Souci, the first Parisian-style cabaret in America, opened in New York in 1915. The San Francisco Ballet was founded in 1935 with the help of Adolph Bolm, a Russian who was one of the stars of the Ballets Russes. Injured during the company's 1917 American tour, he ended up in Hollywood choreographing a John Barrymore film and performing at the Hollywood Bowl before moving to northern California.

Risqué dance and serious ballet came to Las Vegas in their own idiosyncratic ways and almost at the same time. The "Lido de Paris" show opened in 1958 at the Stardust, an attempt to bring some European class to the strip revues; the next year the first bare breasts appeared onstage at the Dunes in a burlesque show. Lou Walters, the director of entertainment at the Tropicana (and father of the television news personality Barbara Walters), combined the two in the same showroom when he staged the "Folies Bergere" in 1959.

That was about the time that Nancy Houssels was graduating from the University of California, Los Angeles as a theater arts student. Houssels, whose height hovers around four-foot-eleven, had appeared in public dance performances as a student. After touring with a Hollywood Bowl show, she auditioned for Francois Szony, a Hungarian who was known as the world's greatest adagio dancer. Adagio consists of combinations of lifts done to slow music, a dramatic way to present ballet in small bites to the masses; it was also referred to as "acrobatic dancing." Although the lifts aren't as dependent on the strength of the man as they appear, it still helps if the female being lifted is smaller rather than larger, and Houssels fit the bill. She was hired and ended up touring on several continents as part of the dance couple known as Szony and Claire.

After an appearance on the Ed Sullivan television show, they were hired in 1964 to dance at the Dunes.

At the same time a Croatian dancer who had escaped from Yugoslavia to London, Vassili Sulich, was working at the Tropicana in its version of "Les Folies Bergere." Hired in 1964 as a principal dancer, he had later been made ballet master. While performing at the Dunes, Nancy Houssels took a class with Sulich to sharpen her technique in the Russian lifts she was doing with Szony. Sulich lured her away to dance in the closing act of the Folies during Christmas 1968. (The same show that also included an early act by two young German magicians, Siegfried and Roy.) She danced for only a few weeks at the Trop before being noticed by Kell Houssels, its president, who, as he tells the story, fell in love with her when he saw her perform and fired her in order to marry her in 1969. Three years later Mrs. Houssels and Sulich put on what was intended to be a one-time-only repertory program at UNLV using dancers from the Strip, many of whom had trained in classical ballet. They sold out the house, and a nonprofit repertory dance company, the Nevada Dance Theatre, was the result.

By the 1980s the company, performing classics of ballet and modern dance, as well as original choreography by Sulich, was touring internationally and receiving grants from the National Endowment for the Arts. A decade later it was the first nonprofit arts organization in the state with an annual budget over a million dollars. Today the company is called the Nevada Ballet Theatre (NBT). It has its own $5-million dance academy and draws principal dancers from other prestigious companies such as the State Theatre of Leningrad, the Kirov, and Korea's Universal Ballet.

Nancy Houssels and I had lunch to talk about the respective roles of showgirls, lap dancers, and ballerinas in Las Vegas, and she confirmed what I'd heard from some of the dancers working the strip clubs: that many of them started out as kids taking ballet lessons. Some even progressed to earning college degrees in dance and performing in local nonprofit dance companies before seeking auditions with the NBT; when they couldn't compete with professionally trained dancers fleeing Eastern Europe and the former Soviet Union, they ended up on the Strip in topless revues (if tall enough) or working in the clubs. Even some NBT dancers, when they become too old for the rigors of ballet, have been known to take up one of the other roles in town.

Houssels, looking at me from under her enormously long eyelashes, a piece of theater carried over from her days as a performer, says: "Dancing in the shows isn't as demanding as ballet, so it's a place they can go. Some of the Strip girls are beautifully trained, but they got too tall . . . and they make better money than we can afford to pay." So the company, which was founded upon the talent of commercial dancers from the Strip, ends up reversing the flow. A final twist in the synergy is that the daughter of an owner one of the larger strip clubs now dances in the company.

There are counterintuitive inversions involved with dance onstage, just as there are with fountains on the Strip. First is that the lap dancers and showgirls are not merely the "quintessential objectified female," as the art historian and critic Libby Lumpkin points out in an essay on showgirls that she wrote while working in Las Vegas as the curator of Steve Wynn's art collection at the Bellagio. She makes the point that the spectacle onstage is a "reciprocal confrontation" in which the showgirl's impassive gaze is met with the longing of the male audience members who wish to be chosen as her mate. Furthermore, when I interview lap dancers, they tell me that they feel more in charge of the relationship when performing in a strip club than when dancing in a corps de ballet, where they find themselves treated like pieces of meat by a ballet master or mistress, who will often yell, taunt, slap, pinch, and otherwise physically and emotionally dominate the young dancers. The gaze of the audience upon the exotic dancer, as it turns out, may not be as invasive as that of a person looking at the exposed underbelly of a lion as he walks overhead on the glass at the MGM.

And what of the role of sex in contemporary ballet? The New York novelist Sigrid Nunez, who took ballet as a young woman and suffered the indignities of the training, put it this way in her novel *A Feather on the Breath of God:*

> It was a long time too before I could watch ballet again, and when I did I was astonished to think I could ever have been so blind. Nothing to do with sex, did I say? Hoisted into the air by her partner, the ballerina is borne downstage, her legs split as wide as they can go, the rushing air driving her chiffon skirt up to her waist. If she is wearing a tutu, the effect is even more startling: a frilly target board with her critch for bull's-eye. There were times, sitting in the dark of the New York State Theater, when it seemed to me that ballet was about nothing *but* sex. (There was a time when the line between dancer and concubine was a thin one. The odalisques of art history were often ballerinas.)

The flow of ideas, people, and money back and forth between the commercial and artistic presentations of dance in Las Vegas, which in some ways parallels that in the presentation of the visual arts in town, suggests two things. First, that the distance between art that receives government support (whether it is grants from the National Endowment for the Arts or a commission from a French queen) and that which earns its way commercially has historically never been that great. This, too, is a productive kind of *frisson*, generating new business models and opportunities as well as aesthetic cross-fertilization. And second, that to try and separate the two with firewalls of regulation would severely hamper the development of both.

Driving down the Strip after the Cirque show, Karen and I pass the marquee at Caesars. Pavarotti is billed to sing at the Colosseum, the hotel's new four-thousand-plus-seat showroom modeled after the fifty-thousand-seat original in Rome. Presumably audiences won't be sacrificing him to some of the local lions, though the critics might, the opera star having long since passed his prime. But he has become a Las Vegas fixture of a sort, his voice on the soundtrack for the Bellagio fountains along with the phrasings of that other notable crooner of Italian extraction, Frank Sinatra. Sharing the marquee with Pavarotti is the gracefully aging British rock idol Elton John.

9

PLOTTING NOT TO PROFIT

Across one wall of Robert Beckmann's living room stands a line of carved African figures atop a row of low bookcases. I'm balancing a cup of coffee on my knee and trying to avoid looking at them. The directors of the Guggenheim-Hermitage and the Las Vegas Art Museum are due in a few minutes, and I'm hungover with images I gathered yesterday.

I started the afternoon by talking with Michele Quinn, the director of the Godt-Cleary Gallery, a new contemporary space at Mandalay Bay currently showing works by the pop artist James Rosenquist. Godt-Cleary is a serious gallery in an upscale shopping mall built into the elevated pedestrian walkway that crosses a street and connects two hotel towers. To say that it is an unusual location for the best art gallery in town would be an understatement in any other city in America. In Las Vegas it's merely common sense, given that it's where the clientele is.

After that I visited some of the strip (small *s*) clubs off the Strip (large *S*) in order to tour their facilities and interview dancers, which of course meant buying martinis for everyone involved, myself included. Then I tottered back here to watch the Oscar Awards over drinks and snacks. I'm still having trouble focusing my thoughts at nine this morning, the vivid images of Rosenquist overlapping with the oil paintings of Rubensian nudes at Treasures, all of them varnished over with a patina of the nostalgia that Hollywood cultivates so assiduously during the annual awards. The last thing I want is to be stared at by somber ancestor figures from Nigeria. Their elongated torsos are based on an ellipse that is centered on the belly button and shaped by their arms with slightly flexed elbows. It gives them a distinct vaginal shape that makes them look, as Beckmann puts it, "like they're turning themselves inside out." My head feels as if it can do that without their help.

What I'm trying to concentrate on this morning is how the shifting values of art might be related to the shifting roles of organizations that present it. It's no news that the value of things changes with context. The African carvings, which tribespeople make as religious and ceremonial objects, are bought by tourists as mementos of their travels, by history museums as traces of belief systems, and by art museums in order to present narratives about the development of early-twentieth-century art. Beckmann buys them to inspire his own work and because he likes to collect things.

When starting to research how J. Paul Getty, Steve Wynn, and other people of wealth collect art, I found a book in the Getty library, *Art on the Market*, published in 1959, by the late French academician and auctioneer Maurice Rheims. He recounts a story that I can't confirm elsewhere, so it may be apocryphal, but it's illuminating nonetheless. The industrialist Henry Clay Frick — robber baron, Andrew Carnegie's partner in the steel business, and widely feared union buster — was one of America's major art collectors at the turn of the last century. In 1912 Frick paid $400,000 for a portrait by Velázquez of Spain's King Philip IV, a known masterpiece by an artist generally conceded to be the greatest of all Spanish painters. When Frick discovered that the king had paid the equivalent of only $600 for the portrait in 1644, he decided to gauge whether he had made a good investment by comparing the current value of the painting with what the original $600 would have come to in 1912 if it had been kept in a bank for the same 268 years. His equation was cosmically oversimplified, calculating only how large that amount would have grown at an annual compound interest rate of 6 percent. The result, when I run the equation, is 605.3 million percent in interest, or something more than $3.6 billion. Rheims does not say whether Frick thought he had gotten a bargain.

Rheims thought that someday an art collector—most likely a Texas oilman, he surmised—would break the $5-million mark for a painting, but that there was a ceiling somewhere to what people would pay. Perhaps. But I wonder what he would have thought of a recent purchase made by the estate of a California oilman. This winter the Getty added a notable painting to its collection of Old Masters, a portrait by Titian of the governor of Milan done in 1533. The *Portrait of Alfonso d'Avalos* shows the bearded warrior encased in armor with a diminutive servant by his side handing him his helmet. D'Avalos was a rich and powerful general in the service of the Holy Roman Emperor Charles V, upon whose authority he had captured the French King Francis I. He was also a politician, and a patron and collector of the arts whose holdings included works by Pontormo and Leonardo. Reputed to have been arrogant, even cruel, he commissioned the leading portrait painter of the time to fashion an image that owes its visual symbols of social hierarchy as much to the Romans as to the Renaissance. His dark armor is ornamented with gold, and he wears the Order of the Golden Fleece around his neck, an ornate collar bestowed by the Habsburgs and signifying the highest knightly honor of the era. His gaze seems imperious, slightly impatient, a psychological undercurrent that helps make the painting one of the great portraits of the Renaissance.

The painting was in the collection of an Austrian count early in the twentieth century before being bought by the Countess Béhague in 1925; she willed it to her nephew, the Marquis de Ganay, whose family kept it until selling off their art collection. The AXA Group, a multinational insurance company founded in France in 1816, bought the portrait in 1990 for roughly $7.6 million, then loaned it to the Louvre for twelve years with the understanding that the French museum could purchase it at any time for that price plus inflation. The Louvre expressed interest in the purchase but inexplicably failed to act, and the Getty plunked down a reported $70 million for it. It is currently the second most expensive Old Master painting ever purchased, its price exceeded only by the $76.7 million sale at Sotheby's in 2002 of *The Massacre of the Innocents* by Peter Paul Rubens.

It intrigues me that the painting, after circulating through the drawing rooms of various wealthy Europeans, ended up at AXA, one of whose divisions is Nordstern Art Insurance, advertised as "the world's leading insurer of fine art and collectibles." Nordstern, which has given both modern paintings and large grants to the Guggenheim Museum and the Museum of Modern Art in New York for a conservation research project, could not help but bask in the symbolic acquisition by the parent corporation, whose worldwide revenues in 2002 exceeded $94.7 billion.

So the likeness of d'Avalos, originally painted both to document his presence and to project that presence as an embodiment of imperial power, becomes a distinguished piece of cultural patrimony that rich Europeans buy to validate their own connections to royalty, which is to say to an undying lineage that is a transmission line of power and privilege. Then it becomes an icon for corporate power. At the Getty it now joins portraits by van Dyck, Rembrandt, Renoir, Cézanne, and others—all artists influenced by Titian—where it resides as a chapter in a massive history of art hung on the walls. I imagine that when Beckmann sees it, he won't be able to resist putting his nose right up to the general's.

It's now become my habit when pondering the collection of either Getty or Wynn to then think of the other one, and the provenance of the Titian leads me to think about Wynn's recent purchase of the 1928 *Odalisque* by Henri Matisse, which is also known as *Oriental Woman Seated on a Floor*. Before the outbreak of World War II the small oil painting of a harem girl in blue pants was in the stock of a prominent Paris gallery owner, Paul Rosenberg, who in addition to being Picasso's dealer also handled work by Matisse, Degas, and Cézanne. After the Nazis invaded Paris in 1940, they confiscated Rosenberg's inventory, and the painting disappeared until 1954, when it mysteriously resurfaced at the Knoedler & Company Gallery in New York. A Seattle lumber tycoon bought it, no questions asked, then donated the painting in 1991 to the Seattle Art Museum.

Rosenberg's descendants, in the meantime, had been tracking down the stolen artworks, and in 1997 they sued the museum for the return of *Odalisque*. After conducting the research required to establish that there was, indeed, no accounting for the whereabouts of the painting from 1941 until 1954, the museum complied and in 1999 gave back the painting to the family, who issued a statement to the press welcoming the return of one of their "children." Within two months they sold the painting to Steve Wynn for a price rumored to be around $2 million.

In this instance, what's interesting is that the Nazis stole what they considered to be a decadent work of art as part of a program to appease their dictator's personal aesthetic ambitions. Hitler had planned on building an art museum in his childhood hometown of

Linz, Austria, a goal presumably related to his early and thwarted strivings to be a painter. To that end, the Nazis swept up more than sixty-one thousand objects in Europe, an estimated one-fifth of the world's total art treasures. When the Rosenbergs sold the painting, the Jewish community was outraged and expressed hopes that the family would at least turn over the proceeds to a fund for victims of the Holocaust. The painting, which measures only eighteen by twenty-two inches, thus assumed a transactional status far beyond a monetary measure.

Attempting to value art in terms of other financial instruments has never worked very well, despite the efforts of economists to compare its long-term appreciation with that of various stock markets. Art remains stubbornly more complicated than a commodity and has no tangible value like grain or gold, or even much status as a fungible instrument standing in for commodities, such as currency. Art considered as a commodity is simply one layer of meaning in the mutlilayered stratigraphy of culture. Art, which has no intrinsic value, is only given value by the community in which it is seen. In turn, it gives value back to that community, whether as an object with educational benefits, one that provides symbolic pride in ownership, or one that serves as a tourist draw. Museums, by maintaining and constantly updating the infrastructure necessary to decode the objects (from stained-glass windows to paintings to video installations), provide access (value) for the society. They maintain our ability to continue a conversation with and about the art, which the Italian philosopher Roberto Casati argues is what makes art valuable, as well as identifiable across cultures.

Furthermore, even the act itself of collecting and interpreting items, be they Old Masters, African carvings, or endangered birds in South America, affects value. The Getty found itself in a quandary when it entered the art market in a serious way during the 1980s. Because its purchasing power far overshadowed that of any other museum in the world, it had to move judiciously in order to avoid unduly inflating the value of paintings, photographs, and other objects that its curators—not to mention those from other museums—wished to purchase from private hands. Although it moved as discretely as possible when bidding on major pieces, prices inevitably rose. This was a situation not unlike that facing Steve Wynn, who likewise acted quietly but whose presence inexorably upped the prices when he started buying in 1996.

∿ Just as the value of items in the collections of art museums and zoos changes over time in relationship to scarcity, historical circumstance, and provenance (expressed with the animals as genetic heritage), so do the roles of the nonprofit organizations presenting those items. And that's what I hope the conversation this morning with Karen Barrett, the current director of the Las Vegas Art Museum, and Elizabeth Herridge, the managing director of the Guggenheim-Hermitage Museum, will shed some light on in the context of Las Vegas.

Barrett, when she arrives, is wearing a gray business skirt suit. A hint of gray streaks her blond hair. She has a background in finance, having worked in New York in estate planning and put together a large trust department for Bank One. Herridge rings the doorbell a few minutes later. She worked on Wall Street as a managing director at Bear, Stearns, earned a degree in connoisseurship at another of the world's leading auction houses, Christie's, and before working at the Guggenheim was an archivist at the LVAM. She has dark hair, wears a long skirt and sweater, and like me is dying for a cup of coffee.

Barrett, who is also an artist and jewelry maker and sells her wares at an exclusive shop in the Bellagio, has come to the conclusion that she needs to do some market research in town. "If people want us to stay out at the library and be small, we need to know that.

But if they want us to build a facility over here, across town, and switch shows between the two every month, we need to know that, too." She is, in short, beginning to frame a strategic long-range plan, which gives me some hope for the future of the organization. If the museum follows that process rigorously, eventually it might find itself in a new facility supported by residents. This isn't a matter of art history, but of business, and she appears equipped to undertake it.

Herridge has a different but related problem, one of getting more locals into the Guggenheim. She admits that perhaps the administration in New York had at first conceived of the Las Vegas branch as being a lucrative venture, but her emphasis is on building a local audience that will use the facility as a real museum and not view it as merely another attraction on the Strip. She's looking for a new education director, more programming with the schools — and ways of working with the LVAM to accomplish that.

"There's an Aztec exhibition coming to New York later this year, and the curators have been talking about us showing some of it here the following year," she says to Barrett. "I think it'd be great, but a lot of the material would be in vitrines, and that doesn't work very well in our space — but it might in yours. I can see people from this region who wouldn't go to New York to see the show, coming here."

"Sure," Barrett replies enthusiastically. "We've begun an outreach program to the local Hispanic community and have had more than three hundred people in on a Sunday to see the Botero show we have up now."

The exhibition by the contemporary Colombian artist is only a show of posters from the Smithsonian traveling exhibition program, and the security and climate controls will need another upgrade in order for the joint program to be feasible, but an offer from the Guggenheim to the local museum is a welcome one. Michele Quinn at Godt-Cleary—a Las Vegas native who worked in New York for more than a decade at places such as Christie's and the Brooke Alexander Gallery—told me that she was starting a collectors' club in town, perhaps doing it in conjunction with Herridge, whose members would be eligible. She was also mulling over starting a salon on Sundays, inviting in local writers and artists to meet with other artists, curators, and art-world notables who might be going through town. That a gallery in a casino, rather than a local art museum, would take on that role is not a development that any amount of cultural planning by a government arts agency would be likely to produce. Barrett mentions that she, too, is interested in starting a club for collectors at the LVAM.

This kind of exchange among a museum in a hotel-casino, a private gallery in another resort, and a nonprofit is still another manifestation of the creativity that it is necessary to exercise in Las Vegas if you want to present either culture or nature in the city. Given the dominance in local capital formation by businesses on the Strip—as well as their political power and will to keep the attention of visitors focused on the resorts—any successful nonprofit has to form alliances with them. That's true whether it is Nancy Houssels at the Nevada Ballet Theatre or Karen Barrett at the art museum.

The blurring of the boundaries between private and public interest that is endemic to Las Vegas continues to present the LVAM's biggest challenge by preventing it from achieving enough curatorial independence to become interesting and respectable. Even as Barrett is attempting to fairly assess community needs, the curator of the museum is planning to give his friend and patron, the former chairman of the board and gallery owner, a retrospective exhibition. That kind of favoritism, however, which stems from the organization's roots as an amateur artists' cooperative, can be construed as a variation on the potential conflict created when the Guggenheim accepts money from a motorcycle company and a clothing company even as it displays their wares.

Such permeability of the barriers between profit and nonprofit makes arts managers nervous, and the current show of Monets at the Bellagio has generated a minor controversy. Following the Warhol exhibition, Marc Glimcher and Andrea Bundonis had the audacity to rent twenty-one of the thirty-six Monets at Boston's Museum of Fine Arts (MFA) and put them on exhibit at the hotel. Peter Schjeldahl and Steve Friess reported in *Newsweek* that the gallery paid an unconfirmed $1-million rental fee. Once Paper-Ball recoups its expenses, the MFA will participate with it in revenues from tickets and merchandising. Schjeldahl was snide about the collaboration, but Christopher Knight at the *Los Angeles Times* was positively apoplectic, asserting that the arrangement violated the code of professional conduct recommended by the Association of Art Museum Directors. The code specifies that when museums make loans, "the intellectual merit and educational benefits, as well as the protection of the work of art, must be the primary considerations, rather than financial gain."

Knight, paraphrasing the urbanist Jane Jacobs, posits museums as "guardian" organizations that exist to protect our cultural heritage. Commercial culture, while not in opposition to guardian culture, has profit as its motive, and Knight believes that when its rules are applied to a guardian organization, a "monstrous hybrid is born," a degraded and unethical situation.

Barrett, Herridge, and Beckmann agree that the show at the Bellagio has educational benefit. The works will be seen by more people in the gallery during the eight-and-a-half-month exhibition than they would in Boston, where they spend most of the time sitting in storage. They are safe, being in the care of art professionals, and the money the MFA earns will help it offset the fact that the total subsidy it receives from the Commonwealth of Massachusetts annually is a paltry $40,000. Malcolm Rogers, the director of the MFA, is a self-confessed admirer of Thomas Krens at the Guggenheim and has sought to brand and expand Boston's museum along parallel lines. If you receive one of the MFA's mail-order catalogs, you know how vigorous a retail operation the museum runs. Rogers defended the arrangement with PaperBall as a way both to reach a larger audience than otherwise possible and to generate revenue. He gave, that is, reasons that were both mission-based and pragmatic.

Furthermore, the history of the MFA is that of a popular museum open free to the public four days a week and which, when it was founded in 1870, presented a mix of high and low artifacts—fine paintings, mummies, Zulu weapons, colored glass, and Christmas cards among them. In subsequent decades the museum's board became the exclusive club of Boston brahmins and the collection was purged of what they considered to be items of low culture, leaving only paintings and sculptures in the gentrified neighborhood of high culture. In the long run this traditional stratification of objects, calculated both to reflect and reinforce hierarchical values in the local society, tends to break down. The larger contextual nature of visual culture is simply too pervasive and compelling to ignore. For example, how do you understand the rise in the monetary and non-tangible values of paintings in New York's Metropolitan Museum of Art without taking into account that they may have appeared on millions of Christmas cards printed and sold by the museum?

Personally, I don't find the MFA's renting paintings to Bellagio any more threatening to the world of art than I find the Vancouver Aquarium's managing Shark Reef detrimental to the future of marine biology. In fact, in many cases it may be preferable for a nonprofit to use its collections and expertise as revenue-generating assets, versus selling itself to corporate bidders or accepting overly restrictive government grants. One of the systemic problems with museums is that their assets are often unbalanced. They have either too many works of art in proportion to the amount of money they have to exhibit them (the case of the MFA and the Guggenheim) or too much cash and not yet enough art (arguably the case at the Getty). Selling off works to one another and renting works to the private sector are obvious solutions still within the bounds of traditional American museum ethics, but ones that museum professionals are slow to embrace, to put it mildly.

The anxieties expressed by Knight and Schjeldahl reflect a wider impulse in the culture toward making more transparent the increasing role played by nonprofits in America, and perhaps even reining in their activities. The largest intergenerational transfer of wealth in the history of the world has commenced as the baby boomers reach retirement and begin to pass away, with correspondingly increased giving to nonprofits quite likely. This generational watershed comes at a time when state and federal lawmakers are examining donations linked to recent corporate scandals and terrorist activities and are demanding increased use of audits so that account books will be more open to both donors and government overseers. The guidelines are also a bureaucratic reaction meant to counter the increasingly apparent effects that for-profit behavior and commercialism are having on how nonprofits do business.

The artists Neil Cummings and Marysia Lewandowska, in their book *The Value of Things*, point out how the roles of department stores and museums have been converging since the introduction of mass production in the mid-nineteenth century. (The philosopher Walter Benjamin had earlier traced the roots of this convergence to the display of commodities in the Paris Arcades from the early 1800s onward.) Both museums and department stores display objects that are classified according to hierarchies meant to satisfy the desires of their customers, and both are built on the assumption that people collect classes of objects, whether those are china plates or contemporary paintings. Collecting inoculates the collector against the loss of memory, yet another small stay against the demands of space and time. Museums capitalize on the impulse with their gift shops — if you can't buy the paintings, then you can at least memorialize the experience of being in their presence with a souvenir. Museums have increasingly become retail destinations, where people spend more time looking at items for sale than at those on exhibition, while retail stores fashion themselves into themed environments that become tourist attractions. The epitome of the crossover in Las Vegas is Caesars Forum, with its shops arrayed around a fountain with animatronic sculptures fashioned to look like Roman antiquities under a changing cloudscape. Among the more than one hundred stores in the themed mall are the Museum Company, which sells reproductions from the Metropolitan Museum of Art and the Museum of Modern Art, and Endangered Species, which offers conservation-themed clothing and collectibles.

Consumers don't have any trouble distinguishing between a museum store and a museum exhibition, or between a Christmas card and the original painting, but that's not to deny that the commercialization of culture is a genuine concern. You wouldn't want people to think that the paintings they see on the cards, for example, are nothing less than crude approximations of reality that photography could make more successfully. To do that would be to deny the diversity of human emotion, thought, and creativity and would severely limit our ability to engage and respond to the world. On the other hand, you wouldn't necessarily want to live in a world without photographs, which bring us different, although sometimes overlapping, categories of information. Having both available, and being able to distinguish between and successfully read them, is a richer range of experience.

I would argue, then, that a myriad of innovative organizations would promote that diversity more effectively than increasingly bureaucratic ones tied up in audits, and the reactions from Knight and Schjeldahl strike me as well intentioned but also neo-Puritanical. Ballet companies did not arise as pristine nonprofits with virgins prancing across the stage, and zoos certainly weren't invented to preserve biological diversity. The country's great museums started out as private collections amassed by wealthy and often unscrupulous businessmen who wished to project an aura of respectability. They worked with connoisseurs such as Joseph Duveen, the art dealer who, starting in 1886 and for five decades thereafter, made a career out of spying upon and opportunistically raiding collections in Europe when their owners were financially disadvantaged, then selling the artworks to the Americans who had plenty of cash but little in the way of cultural heritage.

Duveen sold art and antiquities to millionaires such as Rockefeller, Frick, Mellon, H. E. Huntington, Hearst, and Getty. Ironically, as the most influential transatlantic art dealer from 1910 to 1939, he raised the value of the objects so high that when income and inheritance taxes were implemented, even the richest Americans could no longer afford to buy or bequeath them to their heirs without dire financial consequences. When the United States Revenue Act of 1917 came into effect, allowing tax reductions for charitable purposes, Duveen counseled his clients to pledge their artworks to museums, thus allowing them to continue to afford his offerings. This not coincidentally raised the value of the objects even more.

Nonprofit organizations presenting culture and nature have evolved over time in response to a changing world, whether it was the imposition of income taxes or the increasing scarcity of impressionist paintings and snow leopards. Homogenizing the behavior of the presenting organizations runs counter to their need to respond to those changes. Yes, the separation of power in the marketplace among governmental, for-profit, and nonprofit organizations is, in general, a good thing. It helps create the very diversity by which separate entities can form multiple kinds of relationships. And yes, guidelines meant to maintain public faith in nonprofits help ensure that the public will donate funds to them. But nonprofits presenting nature and culture should be part of the dialogue about the value of their domains, and freezing their ability to be innovative is counterproductive.

The calculated dance between a well-known museum and a famous casino offers more to the two entities than the potential for immediate revenue enhancement. It also has to do with a more subtle strategy of image transfer and co-branding, an upward spiral of name recognition for both of them by combining both corporate presences in the public view. It is in the interests of both partners, however, that the public retain faith in the independence of the two entities; otherwise the value of both is diminished. If the public believes that the museum is no more than a for-profit gallery hawking wares to the highest bidder, then the casino will lose the cultural respectability that the museum as a more credible partner might have brought it. American audiences are quite adept at reading through the facades of simulacra and the machinations of image transfers, just as they recognize product placements of soft drinks and sports cars in movies.

Most nonprofit arts and nature organizations are founded and staffed by people who care deeply about art and the natural world, people who are devoted to exercising and celebrating creativity. That extends not only to the content they present but also to how they do business. They tend to solve problems not just by looking for ways to tighten accounting procedures and control labor costs but by inventing new kinds of organizations and cooperative strategies to accomplish public objectives, whether they're exhibiting art or animals. Put such people in the context of Las Vegas, a city where mainstream social parameters are bent and even violated as a primary way of attracting customers, and you are creating a unique laboratory for experimentation.

I repeat, this is not to say that one would want the nonprofit world to become profit-driven. Supporting educational, cultural, and scientific organizations that set aside profit in favor of mission—not to mention those that provide health care for the sick and elderly and unfortunate—is a critical factor in maintaining a democracy in the face of a consumerist economy. But providing multiple points of access to all of those things without limiting options is vital.

Las Vegas, by virtue of how it has defined its *raison d'être*, must continually reinvent itself in order to meet the desires of audiences for new and unique experiences that cannot be had elsewhere. Doing so enables it to raise enough revenues that it can, in turn, afford to create the next attraction. That's a financial highwire act that you wouldn't want to try in your own hometown, and one that can take place only in a permissive regulatory environment and in an environment so empty of our expectations that it is virtually a blank stage. Those conditions allow a constant repositioning of organizations in the for-profit and not-for-profit sectors that makes Las Vegas a rich environment for diverse business models. And that's healthy in the long run for the culture as whole. Diversity is healthy among organizations just as it is among organic communities.

If the museums are changing their standards in an attempt to bring in wider audiences, and using appearances at the Bellagio to do so, then entertainment venues such as Mandalay Bay are likewise changing their standards by including educational zoological attractions and art galleries to deepen the experiences they offer their clients—a parallel attempt to gain market share. Las Vegas, with its relaxed regulatory environment and ready access to capital, is the ideal setting for such experimentation. In order not to become moribund, societies need places where experimentation can occur, places where people can question accepted business practices and the bounds of taste and ethics, if not of legality itself, and thus open the door for improvements. Yes, there's the corollary: most of the experiments will fail, and some of them will produce results that could be detrimental to your health. Do we stop doing science for the same reasons, or prevent artists from developing new aesthetic models? Of course not.

When Frank Hodsoll was chairman of the National Endowment for the Arts under President Reagan, he asked whether it would be more cost-effective to give the Disney Company grants to make experimental films or to award grants to the individual filmmakers themselves. Hodsoll, who served as chairman from 1981 to 1989, was compelled to ask the question not so much by a desire to streamline the NEA's administrative budget as by a Republican goal in the culture wars: the elimination of, if not all public funding of the arts, then at least NEA grants to individuals. In particular the Republicans wanted to stop public funding for organizations commissioning what certain members of Congress considered to be immoral projects, specifically homoerotic ones such as the exhibition of Robert Mapplethorpe's photographs and the film *Poison* by Todd Haynes, a trilogy of shorts based on the writings of the French author Jean Genet (the film, after receiving $25,000 from the NEA, won the 1991 Sundance Film Festival's Grand Jury Prize).

One of Hodsoll's successors, Bill Ivey, who served as chairman of the NEA under President Clinton, is now asking similar questions—in fact stating that he thinks Michael Kaiser at the Kennedy

Center and Michael Eisner at Disney have issues in common, such as intellectual property rights, the use of technology, and rates of audience participation. Ivey came to the NEA from the Country Music Foundation and had served twice as chairman of the National Academy of Recording Arts and Sciences. Now he is director for the Curb Center for Art, Enterprise, and Public Policy at Vanderbilt University. The center is partially funded by Mike Curb, a wealthy record producer and chairman of a Warner Brothers record division who also once served under President Reagan.

Ivey wants the for-profit and nonprofit sectors to grow as equals and not to take each other as polar opposites, the whining nonprofits pleading poverty while demonizing their rich and venal cousins in the commercial sector. One of his most pressing interests lies in the intersection of copyright law and cultural heritage, a natural enough area given his background, as well as that of Mike Curb—but also one of increasing relevance to the entire spectrum of nature and culture. While Ivey is thinking about the millions of songs and films locked up as corporate assets by Hollywood, some scientists are beginning to wonder about who owns the reproductive rights for the genes of endangered species found only in zoos. Both are potential legalistic bottlenecks in culture and nature.

I am not in favor of the NEA funding Disney to make films. Aesthetic diversity is essential to cultural diversity, and all Mr. Eisner seems to have done is drive the bottom line so relentlessly that he has imperiled the creative life of his own company, which nonetheless in 2003 earned $27 billion without the help of the NEA. But increasingly people are examining the relationships between commerce and culture and wondering if there are ways for the two to support each other and, at the same time, keep the culture open to change.

Sometimes, of course, opportunities for profit arise that lead to a narrowing of cultural options. An example is provided by Clear

Channel Communications, an aggressive and controversial international media conglomerate that owns more than 1,375 radio stations (including four in Las Vegas) and almost 800,000 billboards. Their corporate Web site boasts that they can reach more than half of the adults in America during any working day. In addition to radio and television stations and outdoor advertising spaces, Clear Channel owns most of the large concert venues in the country and tours such megastars as Cher, the Rolling Stones, and Bruce Springsteen—and it has an exhibitions division. More than 80 million people have attended their shows, which are marketed to be blockbusters. To give just two examples, in 2003 Clear Channel Exhibitions opened *Titanic: The Artifact Exhibit* at Chicago's Museum of Science and Industry and *Saint Peter and the Vatican: The Legacy of the Popes* at the Cincinnati Museum Center, the latter a show that featured more Vatican treasures than had ever been seen before in any one place outside of Rome. Both subjects were represented and interpreted through a variety of invaluable artifacts (or their replicas), including art. Here, then, is a for-profit company with annual revenues of nearly $9 billion selling its services to the public through two hundred tax-supported museums and research institutions. Museums cite the need to mount such blockbuster shows in order to keep up public attendance, meaning revenues, but they don't have the financial resources to curate them on their own. In this case, however, museum trustees might consider whether they wish to support a corporation that is under congressional investigation for its ruthless tactics in media consolidation, and one that uses its profits to pay for rallies supporting the war in Iraq—a conflict that has decimated the cultural heritage of one of the oldest civilizations in the world.

The quasi-libertarian economist Tyler Cowen, a professor at George Mason University, argues in his 2002 book *In Praise of Commercial Culture* that art has historically benefitted from the characteristics of free markets, in particular the innovation and feed-back loops fostered by competition, and the surplus of income that a wealthy society puts at the disposal of patrons. He points out how artists from the Italian Renaissance offered their services for hire, as did composers such as Bach, who played weddings and funerals. He traces how artists have benefitted not just economically but also aesthetically from such crossover. Cowen, who is enough of a contrarian to unsettle conservatives as well as liberals, points out that NEA funding may be helpful in helping maintain a diverse culture—but adds that in the long run government funds underwriting the development of the Internet may have done more for artists than direct grants.

One obvious challenge for an art museum in Las Vegas will be to provide audiences with the ability to decode the role of objects in the illusions that the Strip perpetuates, most notably the illusions that we are participating in a locus of wealth and privilege, that we are maintaining some control of our destinies while doing so, and that we are rubbing shoulders with immortality. A museum that could show us how the spectacles of display are used to manipulate audiences and how artworks play a part in creating the requisite veracity would be an interesting institution indeed. And, I have to admit, one that is far more likely than not to be a nonprofit organization with curators sufficiently freed of corporate apron strings.

∿ After my conversation with Karen Barrett and Elizabeth Herridge, I drive back to L.A. to look at some items that might illuminate how we value the collection of culture and nature. I want to track down the lineage of American collections, from the early industrialists to Getty to Wynn, and to see how they fit into the idea of spectacle.

During the years that I've been shuttling back and forth to Las

Vegas from Southern California, the urban waistline of Los Angeles has crept up the Cajon Pass to invade the Mojave Desert, billowing out along I-15 in towns such as Barstow and Victorville and sprawling toward the Nevada border. More recently, Las Vegas has been erupting southward along the same route. First the Strip kept extending itself south toward and then past the airport. Then those hotel-casinos, a discount mall, a power plant, and even a golf course sprouted in Primm at the state line in the Ivanpah Valley—where the new airport will be built. The intervening thirty-five miles, where most of the land is owned by the Bureau of Land Management, is being auctioned off for new subdivisions, strip malls, and master-planned communities superficially themed to look like Mediterranean villages—very much like the ones found in Orange County and the Santa Monica Mountains, in fact.

Las Vegas and Los Angeles aren't going to grow into the same city, but they share more than just the visual style of early motor hotels, subdivisions, and water fountains. Their joint fascination with Egypt is a revealing example. Hollywood appropriated the enthusiasm of the American public for the discoveries made by Howard Carter in 1922 at the tomb of King Tutankhamen and built its own Egyptian Theater the same year. Architects took the theme to Las Vegas with the Dunes and the Sahara, a more recent and elaborate incarnation of which is the Luxor Pyramid.

Opening soon in Los Angeles at the county art museum is Tutankhamen and the Golden Age of the Pharaohs, a return of the funerary items that initiated blockbuster exhibitions as a trend in museums. More than eight million viewers bought tickets to see them as the first King Tut show toured America from 1976 through 1979, and now once again his gold coffin will be displayed in Los Angeles. Egyptian antiquity officials hope that the new four-city tour will raise $40 million toward the construction of a new museum in Cairo. The museum will preserve — what else? — relics from the tombs of the ancient rulers, objects meant for their owners to use in their next lives.

The show is being presented by a subsidiary of the Anschutz Company, which owns the Anschutz Corporation, which owns the Anschutz Entertainment Group, or (AEG) —which owns a laundry list of sports and entertainment companies, including more movie theaters than anyone else (more than six thousand of them, or about 20 percent of all the screens in the country) and Concerts West. The latter company produces the Celine Dion–Franco Dragone extravaganza at Caesars scaled-down replica of the Forum. Philip Anschutz also is the majority stockholder, chairman, or outright owner of such content providers and carriers as Qwest Communications and the *San Francisco Examiner*. Clear Channel must be gnashing its corporate teeth.

Anschutz made his first money in oil, like Getty following his father's footsteps in the business. So what's he doing with King Tut and some of the country's most prestigious museums? Immortality never goes out of fashion, or so I am led to understand.

10

PARADISE UNDERFOOT

It's a foggy winter Los Angeles morning, and I have the Getty Center garden to myself. The trams are not yet running, and the tree-lined zigzag path is deserted as I walk down the small canyon that separates the research institute from the museum. I can't see the pool at the bottom, my vision closely circumscribed by the marine layer drifting over the Santa Monica Mountains and through Sepulveda Pass, but I am surrounded by the sound of a mountain stream sculpted by the designer of the garden, the artist Robert Irwin.

For the last couple of days I've been looking at two exhibitions in town, one of them here at the Getty titled The Business of Art: Evidence from the Art Market. It includes items from the Joseph Duveen archives, which are housed at the research institute, as well as materials by the late German economist Willi Bongard, who in the late 1960s began applying what he termed his *Kunstkompass* to the world's top-selling contemporary artists in order to rank their investment potential. The system, which he mockingly referred to as the *Gloria-Formel*, or "Glory Scale," awarded points to artists according to how many times they were mentioned in certain prominent art journals, which galleries gave them how many shows per year, and what museum collections included them. He plotted two curves for the artists each year, one measuring their accumulation of points, the other the prices of their works sold. If prices for an artist's work rose more slowly than his progress on the point system, then investment potential existed; the larger the gap between the two lines, if both were rising, the higher the potential return.

One of Bongard's Glory Scale graphs is in the show, a faint red grid with a black line climbing steeply upward showing the spectacular rise in the value of Andy Warhol's reputation, and a more modest one representing the prices his prints and paintings were fetching. The artist Bongard ranked as first in investment potential was Robert Rauschenberg. Bongard's system, which independent studies confirm correlates reasonably well to the actions of the art market, is still used widely by collectors in some European countries. Needless to say, both Warhol and Rauschenberg figure prominently in Steve Wynn's collection, although I have no idea if the collector has ever paid any attention to Bongard's system. Presumably Henry Frick, however, would have loved it.

Also in the show is a photograph from 1925 of a sumptuous room in the New York townhouse of the heiress Eleanor Elkins Widener Rice, one of Duveen's best clients. The fully reconstructed eighteenth-century Parisian drawing room cost the widow (whose husband and son had perished on the *Titanic* in 1912) $2 million to assemble. Suzanne Muchnic of the *Los Angeles Times* translates that into $21 million in today's money when adjusted for inflation, or tens of thousands of dollars per square foot.

Duveen, who hired the Paris firm of Carlhian et Fils to re-create period furnishings when originals weren't available, could provide whatever setting was required for the collections of his clients. As the curators of the show point out, this included everything from textiles to porcelains, from light fixtures to wall paneling for "a stately English home, a Gothic chateau, or an eighteenth-century Parisian town house." Duveen also assisted Frick and J. P. Morgan with the domestic accouterments for their treasures, a practice that helped Getty form his own notions of how to create a context for art. As Getty put it in *The Joys of Collecting*, "I firmly believe that beautiful paintings or sculptures should be displayed in surroundings of equal quality." Getty didn't consider fine furnishings as stage props, but as artworks in their own right.

This brings me back to thinking about the great Ardabil Carpet—one of two woven centuries ago—that Getty once owned, the subject of the other exhibition I've recently visited, at the Los Angeles County Museum of Art (LACMA). The design of the Ardabil is based on Islamic paradise gardens—and that fact, in turn, will lead me back to the nature of culture and the culture of nature in Las Vegas.

~~ Sumer, the first known large-scale civilization, began to coalesce around 4000 BC in southern Mesopotamia, an arid region between the Tigris and Euphrates Rivers. As much as 2,500 years earlier, large settlements had existed farther north, where there was greater rainfall—the late neolithic village of Catal Häyük in Anatolia, for example, was an important trading center with six thousand people. But Sumer had the advantage of the two rivers from which irrigation canals could be dug, and it was able to support a cluster of twelve large city-states. Given the increasing aridity of the Near East and the importance of irrigation to sustain its population, it is not surprising that the most profound desire expressed by Sumerians, which was inscribed as poetry on cuneiform tablets, was to find a place of unending water and the eternal peace that could come only when that resource was abundant.

This concept of paradise, derived from the oasis culture of the desert nomads, was made manifest in domestic compounds by rectangles of enclosed greenery across which ran intersecting channels of water—that geometry symbolizing how the divine gift of water from the ground was distributed by hand. This landscaping scheme shows up as early as 4,000 BC on pottery, and almost every major civilization since has built such terrestrial analogs for paradise. The enclosed green spaces and water within rectilinear walls provided shade and coolness but, just as important, exclosed the harsh, arid wilderness from the people. As is often remarked, the word in Old Persian for "garden" stems from that language's word for paradise—*pairidaeza*—which is formed from *pairi* for "around" and *daeza* for "wall."

What we often and somewhat mistakenly call "Persian" rugs encompass a variety of tribal, religious, and commercial textiles made over a 2,500-year span and covering a territory that stretched from current-day Turkey and Iran to China and India. Pre-Islamic rugs knotted by nomadic tribespeople in Central Asia often used design motifs featuring plants and animals, designs that arose from the practice of sympathetic magic meant to ward off evil and ensure fertility. Over time the knots became a kind of writing, and the textiles were used to memorialize significant events in family and local history. The carpets became a way of creating in the desert an increasingly elaborate and civilized stage, a virtual garden in which the owner could welcome guests, negotiate trades, and seduce a lover. When Islam arose in the seventh century, the designs became much more abstract in order to avoid violating religious laws, and small carpets were used as prayer rugs.

As the Mesopotamian cities grew larger, urban carpet workshops sprouted, and they eventually produced rugs that were not only used as furnishings but also prized as investments; a family's entire wealth was sometimes represented by carpets kept in secure storage to appreciate over time. The pinnacle of carpet making occurred in the royal workshops established by rulers of the Shi'ite Safavid Dynasty (1502–1736) in what is now Iran, the reign under which the two Ardabil Carpets were woven in the mid-sixteenth century. The Islamic rulers revived and expanded upon an artistic tradition that included elaborate bookbinding and manuscript illumination, their decorative motifs arising from the foliage of the garden, an intense and organic patterning that seemed to repeat endlessly and represented immortality.

These carpets, with their foliate arabesques constrained within rectilinear borders, are abstracts of paradise gardens and are still considered to be allusions to—and sometimes taken literally to be—gateways to paradise. The Ardabil Carpets, a pair of matched textiles so precious to the Arab world that they were deemed too magnificent for Western eyes to gaze upon for three centuries, feature in their centers a light blue medallion upon which float open lotus blossoms. These pools are bordered by flowering plants, meanders of palmetto and Chinese peonies, which are in turn surrounded by an incredibly complex array of seemingly random vines. In fact, the carpets, which have been analyzed by mathematicians, display a disciplined axial bilateral symmetry, as do the ancient gardens.

The Ardabils apparently came onto the market in the late 1800s only because the temple in which they were housed had suffered extensive damage and funds were needed for its repair. They were acquired by a Manchester carpet broker and quietly shipped to England. One of the carpets had been damaged over time, and part of the lower field and border was removed from the other to repair it, while the latter was partially rewoven and given a new outer border. The first and larger carpet, when exhibited in 1891 in a London gallery, was immediately acclaimed the finest Persian carpet in the world, and renowned figures such as the art critic John Ruskin and the designer William Morris lobbied for its public acquisition. The existence of the other and smaller carpet was kept secret for a few months, lest knowledge of its existence diminish the value of its sibling, but the first was soon sold to the South Kensington Museum (forerunner of the Victoria and Albert Museum) for the equivalent of $4,000.

In 1892 the other carpet was offered for sale to an American millionaire of questionable reputation, Charles Tyson Yerkes, on the condition that he take it out of England. He bought it for the then-astonishing sum of $80,000. Yerkes's collection was sold at auction in New York in 1910, where another American millionaire, the Dutch immigrant Joseph De Lamar, obtained the textile for only $27,000. When Joseph Duveen bought it for $57,000 at an estate sale held upon De Lamar's death in 1919, he made the purchase for his personal collection and subsequently turned down several offers to sell it. In 1931 he lent the great carpet to a prominent exhibition of Persian art in London, then again to a show in Paris in 1938, which is where Getty first saw it. The oil tycoon was immediately captivated by its magnificence and offered to buy the carpet, but Duveen turned him down. Within a few months, however, Hitler's mobilization of the German army and invasion of Poland made the aging connoisseur so nervous that he decided to convert the asset into hard American cash. He sold it to Getty for just under $70,000, a price that the industrialist considered a steal.

The wool and silk carpet is 287 inches long by 161 inches wide, and its total of approximately 35 million knots may have taken a team of six women four years to weave. Its colors were derived from a variety of organic sources, which traditionally included nuts, insects, and plants such as indigo, saffron, turmeric, pomegranates, madder root, and heliotrope. In addition to the richness of the colors used, its woolen strands were dyed one by one, versus in skeins, giving the textile almost infinite variations in shading and tone. Getty valued the carpet as much as had Duveen, even though he placed it on the floor his New York penthouse before having it brought to his residence in Malibu. King Farouk of Egypt offered him a quarter of a million dollars for it in the 1940s, wanting to give it as a wedding gift when his eldest sister married the Shah of Iran, but Getty declined to sell. When he reluctantly donated it in 1953 to the Los Angeles County Museum of Science, History, and Art in Exposition Park—a way for him to offset taxes that year—museum officials called it "the million-dollar carpet." By the time it became part of the Los Angeles County Museum of Art's permanent collection in 1965, you couldn't put a price on it.

The Getty Museum catalog published with LACMA in 1974 to celebrate the gift describes the carpet as giving the viewer "an almost three-dimensional impression" caused by "the fugue-like intricacy of the master design, in which the main medallion with its sixteen ogival appendages appears to float on a field of floral traceries, all this against a vibrant and pulsating blue background of varying tonality." The piece was sent in 1999 to be cleaned by the Royal Textile Conservation Studios at Hampton Court Palace in London, the only facility with a wash table large enough to accommodate it; the cleaning process took nine months. Returned and put on exhibit at LACMA, it now covers much of the floor in the central atrium of the Ahmanson Building. I had last seen it hanging on the wall there in the mid-1990s, and when I walked around it in its new position, I was surprised by how large it is. Viewed up close it almost shimmers, a result of the variations in color and the number of individual knots. When visitors to Getty's penthouse in New York first saw it, it must have paralyzed them with amazement to see such a treasure at their very feet.

The Ardabil Carpet has been treated, in turn, as a political commission, a religious talisman, a convertible asset, a collectible object, a piece of decorative furniture, a potential wedding gift, and now an invaluable treasure of historical art in dialogue with other items in the museum. It is not a traditional paradise garden rug but clearly betrays its origins in its design and in the couplet by the fourteenth-century poet Hafiz that is woven into a cartouche at one end of the carpet:

> *Other than thy threshold I have not refuge in this world.*
> *My head has no resting place other than this doorway.*

The Getty garden is itself somewhat like the Persian carpet, one with multiple natures. It is a work of art but also a decorative space, a park—the Western European version of paradise re-created—and thus a stage for human interaction and where we go to re-create ourselves. People bring lunch to eat on its benches, youngsters roll down the sloping lawns bordering the path, and lovers snuggle in its corners. Yet it represents larger matters, and is a work of contemporary and organic artifice meant to converse with the historical geometry of Richard Meier's austere architecture. Meier himself was originally supposed to design the garden that would embellish the arroyo. Like many people, although I admire his architecture, I am glad that he didn't also fashion the garden. I run my hands along the bronze walls that frame the triangular corners of the walkway, then find one of the weathered teak benches at the bottom from which I can just discern the intricate maze of the pool through the fog.

Meier had his office construct a series of increasingly elaborate models that showed how the garden was to descend in a series of terraces that extended his pristine modernism down the hill. They would terminate in a colonnade that framed a circular reflecting pool, from which the viewer's vision would leap off the horizon and over the city. Here was an obvious allusion to the original Getty Villa—its Roman design in turn inspired by those of ancient Persia, and which enclosed a geometrical garden with a pool in its center. Harold Williams, then president of the Getty Trust, and John Walsh, the director of the museum, feared that so much of one design would overwhelm visitors. They decided that something less severe was required as a counterpoint to and relief from the rectilinear discipline of the buildings. Walsh was beginning to accept that most of the public wasn't going to visit the museum as an educational experience but as a recreational one, and that some space had to be devoted to fulfilling that expectation. As Irwin tells it, he was hired to do battle with Meier, and a contentious struggle was joined.

The prominent California artist designed what he referred to as a "sculpture in the form of a garden aspiring to be art," a slightly geometricized meander that ended in a maze of azaleas that seemed to float in the water. It was a design that Meier detested, and the conflict between the architect and the artist is symbolized in how the plaza and the garden connect. Or don't. On the plaza level a slender stream of water runs along a groove in the top of a long travertine trough, then drops through an aperture into a cavernous amphora shape cut open to the level below. That's the end of Meier's territory. Between the base of the pool that collects the water and the lip of the garden where it begins its descent is a barren strip of dirt that the staff referred to as the "DMZ"—the demilitarized zone—between the work of the two men.

Irwin's design picks up the water and sends it down the hill through a steep rocky waterway, an intimation of wilderness that is crossed repeatedly by the zigzag path that takes you slowly down to the central feature of the garden, three intersecting circles of planters that form a maze in the circular pool that is, in turn, encircled by flowering plants and vines. All of it is framed by Meier's rectilinear architecture. As a result, the pool not only visually evokes the central medallion of a Persian carpet but gives the same emotional release from the surrounding patterns.

～ Collecting—be it carpets, paintings, or tropical fish—is all about desire. It is apparently an atavistic impulse displayed at least as long ago as 80,000 years, the date given to an array of pebbles found in a cave in France, the earliest known such assemblage. Collecting is based on dealing with the world in a unique and hierarchical way by seeking out an opportunity to heighten scarcity. Once you collect something, that denies someone else the ability to own it. Once you collect a number of the same thing, you begin to corner a market of either the actual physical objects or knowledge about them. When you display your collection, you are demonstrating psychological, social, diplomatic, or economic leverage over your peers, whether you're rounding up endangered animals for your menagerie or lining up paintings bought at auction. There are many motives involved when collectors exhibit their treasures, some of them admirable and even charitable—but ultimately they are claiming that they are more important than other people and that their names will last longer by virtue of the scarcity they have created, the power they have exercised in amassing the collection, and the knowledge the objects represent.

The West has long collected the East. The latter's closed societies—China, say, during the time of Marco Polo, or the Near East when Sir Richard Burton collected the stories of Scheherazade—offered supreme opportunities for Western collectors. Not only were their objects difficult (hence expensive and sometimes dangerous) to obtain, but they were inescapably foreign; what was strange provided an opportunity to create spectacle. The more of the strange you collected, the more of a spectacle you could present, which helps explain both the historical British and American fascination with all things Near and Far Eastern, the number of objects from those cultures in Western museums, and the blockbuster exhibitions that they continue to provide, King Tut among them.

The unincorporated town through which 96 percent of the Las Vegas Strip runs is named Paradise, founded in 1950 as an attempt to keep local taxes to a minimum. Despite the fact the initial inspiration for the name stemmed from the Pair O' Dice Club that opened on the old Los Angeles Highway in the mid-1930s, many of the town's early resorts played off the original meaning of the word. Operations such as the Aladdin, the Sahara, and the Dunes amplified the preexisting Arabic desert motif of western motor hotels for their architecture and advertising, playing off the human desire for the exotic, a journey to the edge of experience, and an escape from everyday life. The same impulse created the craze for Orientalism in England during the Victorian era and was continued by Hollywood in movies such as *Sinbad the Sailor,* which was based on a tale in *The Arabian Nights* — translated by Sir Richard Burton and published in the 1880s — a collection of stories that stems from the fictional efforts of Scheherazade to prolong her life. That desire to escape ordinary life by means of the exotic took an even stranger turn when it transmuted Carter's archeological work into a surreal meditation on immortality in a series of movies about mummies and their curses.

The naming of Las Vegas and its resorts acknowledged the desires of the public to collect exotic experiences in a paradise — a walled oasis in the desert — a place that offered a unique combination of sins. Las Vegas is its own kind of garden, and as many writers have noted, a garden is the highest expression of the meeting between culture and nature. The Strip is also a place where time is banished, where the casinos have no clocks. The high walls of the resorts shut out the desert, and inside you wander from fountain to fountain collecting images of faraway cities projected onto a night that is made to shine as brightly as the day. You can order up whatever spectacle you can afford, a pay-as-you-play paradise. The city offers experiences you can't find elsewhere and that you can add to your memory, which is nothing more than a collection of experiences held closely against the march of time. In a consumer society, that which is the strangest and most spectacular is great wealth. Las Vegas enables you not only to gaze upon spectacle but also to sleep in its bed and have sex with it.

The drawing room that Duveen created for Eleanor Widener was a collectible that only her guests were meant to experience (although it was later donated fully intact to the Philadelphia Museum of Art). Like the palatial French classical villa she built with her first husband in Newport, Rhode Island, it was an environment that allowed her to establish equivalency with European royalty, which is to say with blue bloodlines that had staying power throughout the centuries. Las Vegas offers the simulacrum of such experiences on an a mass scale that makes them affordable, and just as Widener bought a mix of real and re-created furnishings, so Las Vegas offers us a fake Venice with real paintings by Italian Renaissance masters. The fact that the spectacle is augmented by genuine artworks helps make it all the more believable as a whole. For Widener, the combination provided a tangible provenance by association to European society; in Las Vegas it increases the illusion that you really are gambling with destiny on the playing fields of the rich and famous. That the illusion can be dangerous and even fatal only adds to the allure. Benjamin Siegel got his head blown off by a Mafia hit man, and Roy Horn almost lost his to a white tiger. Such incidents add to the mystique of Las Vegas; they don't diminish it.

〜 The fog in the Getty garden is burning off in the morning sun, the red petals of the azaleas are beginning to glow, and the first of the day's visitors trickle down the path. Walsh was quite right in assuming that some people would come to the Getty to experience a museum, others to visit a park. While most people choose to peruse the art collection first, others start with the garden, but sooner or later almost all will visit both, wanting to see with their own eyes the interior of the most expensive museum in the world and the treasures it contains, exactly the impulse that Steve Wynn is counting on to make Wynn Las Vegas yet another of his successes.

Las Vegas offers us not only a place where the desert allows and even encourages the construction of an experiment but also a place to learn about the nature of reality and the reality of nature through the naked stratigraphy of its culture. And that, in turn, allows us to understand more about the role that museums and zoos play in our lives. Several authors have noted that the Strip has evolved along the lines of the European *Wunderkammern,* or "wonder cabinets," assembled by royalty during the sixteenth and seventeenth centuries. Precursors to the museums and zoos of today, these collections featured both *naturalia* (fossils, mineral specimens, stuffed animals from faraway lands) and *artificialia* (artworks and scientific instruments) and were meant to educate as well as to entertain. The dialogue between the two classes of objects offered up a bizarre surrealism at times, the finger joints of saints resting beside miniature wind-up automata, precious jewels sitting next to dinosaur bones. The premiere American example was the Peale Museum in Philadelphia, which some claim to have been our first national museum.

Charles Willson Peale, who lived from 1741 to 1827, was a noted portrait painter and in 1782 built a long exhibition gallery onto his house to showcase his pictures of notable Americans. Peale was also, however, a gifted naturalist and in 1801 excavated two mastodon skeletons, a feat he later memorialized in a large history painting, *The Exhumation of the Mastodon* (1806–08). When he assembled one of the remains later that year, it became the first mounted fossil skeleton in America. The next year he moved his collections of art and natural history specimens onto the second floor of what is now Independence Hall in Philadelphia. Sea captains brought him animals from all over the world that he kept in his own personal open-air zoo, learning taxidermy in order to mount their carcasses for exhibition after they died.

The museum, which eventually exhibited seven hundred birds and four thousand species of insects, also showed paintings, furniture, books, and wax figures of North American Indians posed with their weapons. Peale had started the museum as a money-making venture to support himself and his family, and although he often sought public funding, he received almost none. As a result, he was careful to offer such crowd-drawing curiosities as tattooed human heads and a deformed cow. A gift shop provided a printed guide to the collections, as well as souvenirs for sale. Twenty-two years after Peale's death, the pioneer of commercial American spectaculars, P. T. Barnum, bought the collection to add to his American Museum in New York.

The museum made Peale enough money that in 1810, when he was sixty-nine years old, he could afford to buy a 104-acre farm outside the city and leave the running of the institution to one of his sons. While Widener was building Miramar, her Newport estate, Peale was sculpting the landscape at Belfield. He based its design on his study of landscape paintings and imitated William Hogarth's sinuous recurving lines for his paths. The garden was dedicated both to the study of scientific principles applied to agriculture and to the aesthetics of a park made to imitate and illuminate the principles ordering nature. Peale corresponded frequently with his friend Thomas Jefferson, whom he had appointed as the head of his museum board. The ex-president was likewise a dedicated gardener and polymath, and in an 1812 letter to him Peale exclaimed, "Your garden must be a Museum to you." In reality, however, it was Peale who had created another kind of museum in the country.

Peale would have understood both the evolving presentation of spectacle in Las Vegas and the exhibition of scholarship at the Getty Center. He would have had no trouble accepting that resorts in Las Vegas could successfully exhibit animals and art as attractions, and whether the latter was bought from William Acquavella, the New York dealer in blue-chip impressionist artworks, or rented from the Boston Museum of Fine Art would not have troubled him. Likewise, he would not have found it bothersome that animals on the Strip were presented as players in a magic act or research subjects administered by a nonprofit entity such as the Vancouver Aquarium. I imagine he would have admired the Getty both for its art and its garden and would have been intrigued by the business models emerging among the profit and nonprofit sectors in Las Vegas. After all, he cultivated the seeds of all these things at his own museum and at Belfield. And as a gardener, perhaps he would have noted that the floral designs of carpets in the casinos and the way their repeating runs of curling tendrils are contained within the rectilinear confines of the gaming areas bear more than a passing resemblance to the patterns of the Ardabil Carpet. The vines of both seem to wind into infinity, as if to imply an unending life.

Museums conserve the past for the future; zoos attempt to ensure the viability of species through time; dance with all its sexual overtones is tied intimately to the perpetuation of our own species. And art itself? The oldest known evidence we have for it as of 2004 comes from 307 pieces of pigment found in a cave in Zambia, pieces brought from miles away and then ground into powder, presumably used to decorate the bodies of the pre—*Homo sapiens* 400,000 to 350,000 years ago. Or perhaps it is a stone, unearthed in Morocco, that looks like a crude human figure, bears traces of what may have been pigment, and has been dated to 400,000 years before present. As ancient as it is, scientists cannot tell definitively yet if it is an artifact of culture or a geofact of natural processes, such as weathering. The oldest known art object for now, therefore, remains the Vogelherd horse, a two-inch miniature carved from mammoth tusk during Ice Age Germany more than 32,000 years ago. The oldest pieces in the Getty collection? Small terracotta females fashioned by anonymous hands in Neolithic Greece between 6000 and 4000 BC and commonly taken to be fertility figures.

Art, though, is mortal. It breaks, burns, decays; it's thrown out in the trash, blown up in wars, and buried never to be found again. Ancient Greek literature contains mention of thousands of sculptures and paintings, yet none of the paintings survive, and only twenty-four sculptures from a seven-hundred-year period are clearly attributed to individual sculptors. When the Moghuls invaded Persia during the thirteenth century, the first six centuries of Islamic painting disappeared. More than 90 percent of medieval manuscripts have been lost. Even such a popular and recent genre as eighteenth-century Dutch painting had suffered a loss in excess of 90 percent by the end of that one-hundred-year period. Art can outlast humans and is sometimes the only evidence left of entire civilizations, but it is hardly immortal.

What lasts is the desire itself to leave some trace of ourselves indelibly in the world, and we keep looking for new ways to fulfill it. Museums and churches have that in common, and it's long been claimed that Las Vegas has more churches per capita than any other city in America—an urban myth, but the city does have hundreds of houses of worship, along with wedding chapels. Our genetically based drive to touch immortality seeks manifold ways toward satisfaction, and no doubt we will continue to invent new methods to institutionalize the illusion of the experience, which will continue to challenge the barriers between the nonprofit and for-profit presentation of spectacle.

～ I am still thinking of Steve Wynn looking up at the undersea garden Dale Chihuly mounted in the lobby of the Bellagio and asking for more. And I ponder his purchase of the *Odalisque* by Matisse and his desire to name his new resort after *Le Rêve*, the sinuous portrait that Picasso painted in 1932 of Marie-Thérèse Walter, his twenty-two-year-old mistress, which some critics have called the *Mona Lisa* of the twentieth century. The painting was purchased by the New York couple Victor and Sally Ganz in 1941 for $7,000, their first purchase in what ended up as the largest private holding of Picassos in the country. They hung it in their den over a sofa and coffee table. When their collection went on sale at Christie's in 1998, Wynn paid $48.4 million for the painting. It has been said that he is more fond of it than anything else in his collection, but I wonder if it is for sale to the right bidder, or if it will be included someday in a bequest to a museum. I wonder if, once the Mirage and Bellagio and Wynn Las Vegas resorts are imploded to make way for new buildings—just as Wynn took down the Desert Inn—he will be remembered at all unless it is through the paintings that have passed through his hands.

Our hopes are wild imaginings,
Our schemes are airy castles,
Yet these, on earth, are lords and kings,
And we their slaves and vassals;
Your dream, forsooth, of buoyant youth,
Most ready to deceive is;
But age will own the bitter truth,
"Ars longa, vita brevis."

Adam Lindsay Gordon, from *Ars Longa (A Song of Pilgrimage)*

The eternity of art becomes a metaphor for the eternity of the soul. . . . The industry of the Absolute Fake gives a semblance of truth to the myth of immortality through the play of imitation and copies, and it achieves the presence of the divine in the presence of the natural. . . . The ideology of this America wants to establish reassurance through Imitation. But profit defeats ideology, because the consumers want to be thrilled not only by the guarantee of the Good but also by the shudder of the Bad. . . . Thus, on entering his cathedrals of iconic reassurance, the visitor will remain uncertain whether his final destiny is hell or heaven, and so will consume new promises.

Umberto Eco, *Travels in Hyperreality*

AFTERWORD

As I mentioned in the preface, narrative scholarship is told through the device of a journey. Writers in this genre tend to hew closely to the physical circumstances of their trip in order to form both a coherent story and a consistent analysis. Likewise, we usually keep the book within the time frame of the actual travel in an effort to preserve unity. But because there is a lag of at least a year between writing and publishing, the subject under discussion can change. In the case of Las Vegas, its very economics are dependent upon change. Its primary industry is based on servicing desire, a notoriously a fickle condition. Satisfy it one way and it demands something new to fixate upon.

I started thinking about this book in spring 2002 and am writing these final words in winter 2004; you will be reading the book about a year after this afterword was written. The particulars of the relationships among the for-profit, not-for-profit, and government sectors will have continued to evolve in Las Vegas, but the underlying dynamics will remain much the same. This afterword is provided as a reminder of how powerful that dynamic is, and to emphasize that the significance of the particulars is to reveal the larger forces that create them.

The libertarian tax structure of Nevada won't have changed much, if at all, because visitors will still be paying the majority of the taxes. The number of people visiting Las Vegas to satisfy their desires through the illusion of control over destiny—whether it is in the cards or the services of a call girl—will continue to increase. Because the desire for immortality is met only with illusions and therefore never really satisfied, visitors will return to the Strip for another fix as long as the illusions remain compelling—and that means asymptotically approaching new levels of realism. As long as the synergy between Hollywood and Las Vegas in developing new entertainments remains profitable, that feedback loop will continue to deepen.

The most important change on the Strip is clear evidence of that dynamic. In June 2004 Kirk Kerkorian's MGM Mirage announced that it was acquiring the Mandalay Resort Group for $4.8 billion. Although antitrust regulators may require Kerkorian's company to divest itself of a casino or two, the initial deal would give him control of almost 50 percent of the Strip—eleven hotels, including the Bellagio and Mandalay Bay, and something like 36,500 rooms. The MGM group will now have a $750 million projected annual cash flow to once again reinvent the street in any way it wants. Their opening salvo consists of a proposal to create a $3–4 billion multiuse urban metropolis on the Strip, using a sixty-six-acre parcel to erect hotels, retail malls, and condos. That is, they are building a city within a city.

In response, the Harrah's Entertainment people announced in July that they were buying Caesars, which would then give them command of six major players on the Strip, including the Flamingo and the Rio. That's about 20 percent of business on the Strip, and the $9.5 billion move will make Harrah's the largest gaming corporation in the world, with 95,000 employees at its more than fifty gaming properties scattered from Las Vegas to Atlantic City.

The reaction of people such as Hal Rothman at UNLV, David McKee writing in *Las Vegas Weekly*, and myself is to wonder if this tectonic shift in ownership means the level of innovation on the Strip will decrease. Unlike the corporations run by Wynn and Adelson, which are direct reflections of their founders' personalities, the larger corporations tend to be run by committees of accountants and attorneys. That may increase management skills, but it usually lowers allegiance to creativity. Once Harrah's bought the Rio, for example, the hotel stopped adding to its art collection. Already the Godt-Cleary Gallery has opened an annex in the tiny downtown arts district, which hosts the best of the locally based contemporary art galleries in town. It is only logical to speculate that the gallery might move out of Mandalay Bay altogether. Whether the gallery could sustain itself apart from the Strip is anyone's guess.

Not far from the arts district is a sixty-one-acre parcel the city is developing, within which it has reserved space for a possible performing arts center. The board of directors for the center just received a feasibility study suggesting that a theater large enough to accommodate Broadway shows should be included in the complex. They're years behind the curve. Wynn Las Vegas has secured rights to the year's winner of the Tony Award for best Broadway show, *Avenue Q*, and is building a $40-million theater for it in the hotel. Instead of touring the country after its initial run in New York, the show will appear exclusively in Las Vegas, lowering the costs substantially for the producers while simultaneously increasing the audience. This unheard-of arrangement shocked major nonprofit performing arts presenters across the country, which often count on first-run Broadway shows as a financial staple.

Franco Dragone's new show will still appear in a separate custom-built showroom elsewhere in the hotel. It's a water-based entertainment utilizing a 1.5-million-gallon performance tank and carrying the name "Le Rêve." Agents from Cirque du Soleil were spotted at the Olympics in Athens looking for new gymnastic talent—which created some press over the separation of amateur and professional (that is, nonprofit and for-profit) athletes. There's talk of a *Zumanity* cabaret opening in New York. Furthermore, Clear Channel is producing a shortened but apparently lavish version of *Phantom of the Opera* as a permanent attraction at the Venetian Resort in Las Vegas. The *New York Times* is asking whether Las Vegas will become the next Broadway, and Wynn now touts Las Vegas as the up-and-coming premier performing arts venue in America.

In terms of the visual arts market, an early and relatively minor Picasso painting sold for more than $104 million, almost doubling the previous record price paid for a work by the artist—and moving the title for the most expensive painting in the world forward from the impressionist era into the modernist one, a predictable state of affairs, given the increasing scarcity of paintings from the former period. Eventually the evolution of marketplace prices will be reflected in the increasing attention the public will devote to modern art. It's not public taste driving up the prices, but scarcity, which in turn will shape public desire to participate.

In the meantime, however, the last Vermeer to be authenticated in contemporary times, *Young Woman at the Virginals,* was sold to an anonymous phone bidder at Sotheby's in London for $30 million, the only Vermeer to appear at auction since 1921. Wynn is the reputed buyer, although he has neither confirmed nor denied the report. In November Wynn imploded the last remaining building from the Desert Inn, having two months earlier sent his art collection to Reno for temporary exhibition at the Nevada Museum of Art, the only other art facility in the state besides the Guggenheim that is accredited by the American Association of Museums.

Nevada's governor declared a state of emergency based on the five-year drought, the worst in the western United States since the 1500s according to tree-ring analysis. Pat Mulroy at the Las Vegas Valley Water District has initiated steps to build a $2-billion network of pipes from groundwater wells to the north in rural Nevada, the largest public works project in the state since Hoover Dam. Congress approved a bill establishing the necessary utility corridor from the northern counties in November 2004. Mulroy's goal is to lower the city's dependency on Colorado River water from 90 to 60 percent through the transfer of the fossil water and local conservation. Mulroy says that there is no reason for Las Vegas to run out of water or to stop growing—but that avoiding the one and allowing the other will require shifting from the least expensive source to the most expensive. Water is still, apparently, flowing uphill toward money.

Roy Horn, although paralyzed on his left side, was able to stand up from his wheelchair in August. Although the Siegfried & Roy show on the Strip is no more, NBC broadcast several episodes of a prime-time cartoon show based on the backstage life of the entertainers' white lions. The computer-generated animation series from Dreamworks, *Father of the Pride*, was of "film quality," each episode costing $1.6 million to make. In order to make the potential television audience more comfortable with the mauling of Horn, a new version of the event was circulated in Hollywood. Montecore apparently became fascinated with the beehive hairdo of a woman sitting in the front row and lay down onstage to get a better look. Horn stumbled when bending down to the big cat, whereupon Montecore thought his master was in jeopardy and dragged him off to safety behind the curtain. This attempt to suppress the fact that wild nature could violently overcome the power of the trainer (hence of illusion of the Strip itself) met with skepticism in some quarters. The series was canceled after the first few episodes aired.

The newest Cirque du Soleil show, scheduled to open in 2005, is *Kà* at the MGM, a $165-million extravaganza that is being billed as virtually a live movie. (The cost itself is more in line with a blockbuster movie than a theatrical event—the total cost of all shows opened on Broadway the previous year was only $135 million.) Featuring seventy-two performers, this Egyptian-themed epic is basically a martial arts spectacular that is a Cirque first—it follows a storyline and a single viewpoint, both cinematic conventions. Vertical battle scenes, a forty-two-voice chorus, flying fireballs, and a 230,000-pound gantry lifting stage components above the audience are all deployed to follow the fate of twin sisters separated in battle. And the title? *Kà* is the ancient Egyptian word for what we might translate as "immortal soul." It was the reason that Egyptians had their bodies mummified—so that one's *Kà* would always have a place to live.

BIBLIOGRAPHY

The conversations among cultural critics, arts administrators, policy analysts, environmentalists, and nature scholars are both deep and broad, although the groups don't talk to each other as often as they might. A bibliography for the combined discussions would be immense, and I have listed here only those sources directly influencing the text.

Alexander, Victoria D. *Museums and Money: The Impact of Funding on Exhibitions, Scholarship, and Management.* Bloomington: Indiana University Press, 1996.

Andy Warhol: More Than Fifteen Minutes. Exhibition catalog. Las Vegas: Bellagio Gallery of Fine Art, 2003.

"Art Rental and Licensing Agreement" between Steve Wynn and Wynn Resorts. http://contracts.corporate.findlaw.com/agreements/wynnresorts/wynn.art.2001.11.01.html.

Barnes, Sally. *Female Bodies on Stage.* London: Routledge, 1998.

Baumol, William J. "Unnatural Value: Or Art Investment as Floating Crap Game." *American Economic Association Papers and Proceedings* 76:2 (May 1986): 10–14.

Belk, Russell W. *Collecting in a Consumer Society*. London: Routledge, 1995.

Berman, S. N. *Duveen*. New York: Random House, 1951.

Boje, David M. "Las Vegas Striptease Spectacles: Organization Power of the Body." In *Business Research Yearbook: Global Business Perspectives*, vol. 7, edited by Jerry Biberman and Abbass Alkhafaji. Saline, MI: McNaughton and Gunn, 2000.

Caves, Richard E. *Creative Industries: Contracts between Art and Commerce*. Cambridge, MA: Harvard University Press, 2000.

Clotfelter, Charles T., and Thomas Ehrlich, eds. *Philanthropy and the Nonprofit Sector in a Changing America*. Bloomington: Indiana University Press, 1999.

Cowen, Tyler. *In Praise of Commercial Art*. Cambridge, MA: Harvard University Press, 2002.

——. "Venture Capitalism: Investment Ideas for Mixed For-Profit, Non-Profit Partnerships," in *Building Creative Assets: New Ways for the Entertainment and Not-for-Profit Arts to Work Together*. Washington, DC: Americans for the Arts, 1998.

Cronin, William, ed. *Uncommon Ground: Rethinking the Human Place in Nature*. New York: W. W. Norton, 1995.

Cummings, Neil, and Marysia Lewandowska. *The Value of Things*. Basel: Birkhaüser, 2000.

Davis, Mike. "Las Vegas Versus Nature." In *Reopening the American West*, edited by Hal Rothman. Tucson: University of Arizona Press, 1998.

Debord, Guy. *Society of the Spectacle*. Detroit: Black and Red, 1983.

De Marchi, Neil, and Crawford D. W. Goodwin, eds. *Economic Engagements with Art*. Durham, NC: Duke University Press, 1999.

Denton, Sally, and Robert Morris. *The Money and the Power: The Making of Las Vegas and Its Hold on America*. New York: Vintage, 2002.

Didion, Joan. "The Getty," in *The White Album*. New York: Simon and Schuster, 1979.

DiMaggio, Paul J. *Nonprofit Enterprise in the Arts: Studies in Mission and Constraint*. New York: Oxford University Press, 1986.

Eco, Umberto. *Travels in Hyperreality*. New York: Harcourt Brace, 1986.

Farquharson, Alex, ed. *The Magic Hour: The Convergence of Art and Las Vegas.* Ostfildern, Germany: Hatje Cantz, 2002.

Feldstein, Martin, ed. *The Economics of Art Museums.* Chicago: University of Chicago Press, 1991.

Friess, Steve, and Peter Plagens. "Show Me the Monet." *Newsweek,* January 26, 2004.

Getty, J. Paul. *The Joys of Collecting.* New York: Hawthorn Books, 1965.

Goldstein, Malcolm. *Landscape with Figures: A History of Art Dealing in the United States.* New York: Oxford University Press, 2000.

Gottdiener, Mark. *The Theming of America: Dreams, Visions, and Commercial Spaces.* New York: Westview Press, 1997.

Hancocks, David. *A Different Nature: The Paradoxical World of Zoos and Their Uncertain Future.* Berkeley: University of California Press, 2001. Among the sources I consulted about the collection and exhibition of animals, this is the book to which I owe the largest debt.

Hannigan, John. *Fantasy City: Pleasure and Profit in the Postmodern Metropolis.* London: Routledge, 1998.

Hansen, Maia. "Skin City." In *The Real Las Vegas: Life beyond the Strip,* edited by David Littlejohn, 217–42. New York: Oxford University Press, 1999.

Hanson, Elizabeth. *Animal Attractions: Nature on Display in America's Zoos.* Princeton, NJ: Princeton University Press, 2002.

Haskell, Frances. *The Ephemeral Museum: Old Master Paintings and the Rise of the Art Exhibition.* New Haven, CT: Yale University Press, 2000.

Heilbrun, James, and Charles M. Gray. *The Economics of Art and Culture.* New York: Cambridge University Press, 2001.

Hess, Alan, Denise Scott Brown, and Robert Venturi. *Viva Las Vegas: After-Hours Architecture.* San Francisco: Chronicle Books, 1993.

Hickey, Dave. "A Home in the Neon." *Air Guitar: Essays on Art and Democracy.* Los Angeles: Art Issues Press, 1997.

Johnson, Mike. "Siegfried & Roy Timeline." *Las Vegas Review-Journal,* October 12, 2003, 5-E.

Jowitt, Deborah. *Time and the Dancing Image.* Berkeley: University of California Press, 1989.

Kinetz, Erika. "How Much Is That Dancer in the Program?" *New York Times*, August 15, 2004, 2-1.

Kinsella, Eileen. "Don't Waste the Deduction." *ARTnews* 101 (September 2002): 128–31.

Klein, Norman M. *The Vatican to Vegas: A History of Special Effects.* New York: New Press, 2004.

Knight, Christopher. "Public Trust, Private Gain." *Los Angeles Times*, February 15, 2004, E-40.

Kuspit, Donald. "The Problem of Art in the Age of Glamor," in *Signs of Psyche in Modern and Postmodern Art.* New York: Cambridge University Press, 1993.

Learmount, Brian. *A History of the Auction.* London: Barnard and Learmount, 1985.

Lenzner, Robert. *The Great Getty: The Life and Loves of J. Paul Getty— Richest Man in the World.* New York: Crown, 1985.

Littlejohn, David. *The Real Las Vegas: Life beyond the Strip.* New York: Oxford University Press, 1999.

Lumpkin, Libby. "The Showgirl," in *Deep Design: Nine Little Art Histories.* Los Angeles: Art Issues Press, 1999.

Lumpkin, Libby, ed. *The Bellagio Gallery of Fine Art: Impressionist and Modern Masters.* Las Vegas: Bellagio Gallery of Fine Art, 1998.

Martin, Steve. *Kindly Lent Their Owner: The Private Collection of Steve Martin.* Las Vegas: Bellagio Gallery of Fine Art, 2001.

Meyer, Karl Ernest. *The Art Museum: Power, Money, Ethics: A Twentieth Century Fund Report.* New York: Morrow, 1979.

Moehring, Eugene. *Resort City in the Sunbelt: Las Vegas, 1930–1970.* Pbk. Reno: University of Nevada Press, 1995.

Muchnic, Suzanne. "Going to Market." *Los Angeles Times,* March 21, 2004, E-36.

Nunez, Sigrid. *A Feather on the Breath of God.* New York: HarperCollins, 1995.

O'Neill, Mark. "The Good Enough Visitor." In *Museums, Society, Inequality,* edited by Richard Sandell, 22–40. London: Routledge, 2002.

Parker, Alan Michael. "Finding Luck, Seeking Virtue in the New Las Vegas." *Common Review* 2:2 (Spring 2003): 6–13.

Ratcliff, Carter. "The Marriage of Art and Money." *Art in America* 76 (July 1988): 76–85, 145–47.

Rectanus, Mark W. *Culture Incorporated: Museums, Artists, and Corporate Sponsorship.* Minneapolis: University of Minnesota Press, 2002.

Rheims, Maurice. *Art on the Market: Thirty-five Centuries of Collecting and Collectors from Midas to Paul Getty.* Translated by David Pryce-Jones. London: Weidenfeld and Nicolson, 1959.

Richardson, Edgar E., Brooke Hindle, and Lillian B. Miller. *Charles Willson Peale and His World.* New York: Abrams, 1982.

Rothfels, Nigel. *Savages and Beasts: The Birth of the Modern Zoo.* Baltimore: Johns Hopkins University Press, 2002.

Rothman, Hal. *Neon Metropolis: How Las Vegas Started the Twenty-First Century.* London: Routledge, 2002.

Rugoff, Ralph. *Circus Americanus.* London: Verso, 1995

Sandell, Richard, ed. *Museums, Society, Inequality.* London: Routledge, 2002.

Schjeldahl, Peter. "Helluva Town." *Art issues* 46 (January–February 1997): 14–19.

Schwartz, Gary. "Ars Morendi: The Mortality of Art." *Art in America,* November 1996, 72–75.

Scott, Carol. "Measuring Social Value." In *Museums, Society, Inequality,* edited by Richard Sandell, 41–55. London: Routledge, 2002.

Secrest, Meryle. *Duveen: A Life in Art.* New York: Alfred Knopf, 2004.

Shell, Marc. *Art and Money.* Chicago: University of Chicago Press, 1995

Spanier, David. *Welcome to the Pleasuredome: Inside Las Vegas.* Reno: University of Nevada Press, 1992.

Stead, Rexford. *The Ardabil Carpets.* Malibu, CA: J. Paul Getty Museum, 1974.

Thomas, Helen. *Dance, Modernity and Culture: Explorations in the Sociology of Dance.* London: Routledge, 1995.

Thompson, Hunter. *Fear and Loathing in Las Vegas: A Savage Journey to the Heart of the American Dream.* 1972. Reprint, New York: Vintage, 1989.

Tully, Judd. "Trading Aces." *Art + Auction* 26 (November 2003): 128–34. A profile on the reclusive José Mugrabi.

Venturi, Robert, Denise Scott Brown, and Steven Izenour. *Learning from Las Vegas.* Cambridge, MA: MIT Press, 1977.

Walsh, John, and Deborah Gribbon. *The J. Paul Getty Museum and Its Collections: A Museum for the New Century.* Los Angeles: J. Paul Getty Museum, 1997.

Weiss, Philip. "Selling the Collection." *Art in America* 78 (July 1990): 124–31.

Weschler, Lawrence. *Boggs: A Comedy of Values.* Chicago: University of Chicago Press, 1999.